HOMOSEXUALITY
IN THE ORTHODOX CHURCH

"I entreat you, O Virgin,
Disperse the storm of my grief,
and the soul's most inward confusion,
Scatter it far from me;
You are the Bride of God,
For you have brought forth the Christ,
the Prince of Peace;
Only, all-blameless One."

— *excerpt from the Service of the Small Paraklesis*

HOMOSEXUALITY
IN THE ORTHODOX CHURCH

EDITED BY JUSTIN R. CANNON

Homosexuality in the Orthodox Church
Edited by Justin R. Cannon

Homosexuality in the Orthodox Church Copyright © 2011 by Justin R. Cannon. All Rights Reserved.

Contributing authors have given expressed permission to print their essays in this anthology. Authors whose work appears herein retain all legal rights including copyrights to their individual works.

Without limiting the rights under copyright reserved above, no part of this publication may be reproduced, stored in or introduced into a retrieval system, or transmitted, in any form or by any means (electronic, mechanical, photocopying, recording, or otherwise), without the prior written permission of the editor of this book.

Cover image copyright © Vladamir Wrangel - Fotolia.com.

ISBN: 978-1456416874
First Edition.
www.gayorthodox.com

ABOUT THE EDITOR

JUSTIN R. CANNON is the founding director of Inclusive Orthodoxy (www.InclusiveOrthodoxy.org), an affirming outreach ministry to lesbian, gay, bisexual and transgender, and transsexual Christians centered on his study *The Bible, Christianity, & Homosexuality*, an analysis of the scriptures often used to condemn gays and lesbians. He received his Bachelor of Arts from Earlham College, and graduated with a Master of Divinity from Church Divinity School of the Pacific in Berkeley, California.

Justin hopes for the day when Inclusive Orthodoxy is the norm and partnered lesbian, gay, bisexual, transgender, and transsexuals may be received openly into the full sacramental life of the Orthodox churches.

TABLE OF CONTENTS

Preface   11

Personal Testimony*
    I.   Helena   15
    II.   Barry   21
    III.   Matthew   29
    IV.   Elizabeth   39

From the Bishop's Desk   45

A Brief History   79

Study of the Holy Scriptures   87

Resources   115

* These names have been changed to protect the authors' anonymity.

PREFACE

Throughout Jesus' ministry, he challenged cultural and religious beliefs that excluded, shut out, or devalued any human being. In a culture where tax collectors were corrupt and despised, he broke bread with them and shared a meal. The Pharisees were confused by this and exclaimed, "Why does your teacher eat with tax collectors and sinners?" (Matthew 9:9-13)

In a world of innumerable purity laws and cultural norms that governed interactions between Jews and Gentiles, as well as between men and women, Jesus asked a Samaritan woman for a drink of water. She exclaimed, "How is it that you, a Jew, ask a drink of me, a woman of Samaria?" (John 4:1-42)

Wherever he went, Jesus broke taboos and cultural boundaries that dehumanized people. He gave attention to the outcasts of society—the sick, the handicapped, and even those who were demonically possessed. He showed the greatest concern for those on the fringe of society, particularly the poor and marginalized. Quite regularly, he even confronted those in power who considered themselves to be superior to others.

In Jesus' time, the testimony of a woman was not valid in Jewish courts, yet he chose women to be the first witnesses of the Resurrection and sent them to proclaim the Resurrection to the disciples. (John 20:1-18; Matthew 28:1-20)

Perhaps the most succinct expression of Jesus' scandalous ministry is his invitation, "Come unto me *all* you who are heavy laden and I will give you rest." (Matthew 11:28)

The radically inclusive message of the Gospel has been perverted over the years, as the Bible has been used to support slavery, segregation, racism, anti-Semitism, and sexism. Jesus' ministry, however, witnesses a faith that extends an invitation to all.

Following in the footsteps of Christ's ministry to the outcasts and marginalized, how can the Church faithfully minister to homosexual Orthodox Christians? Too many of our brethren have been ostracized from their churches and homes after sharing about their sexual orientation. Surely, there is a more loving response.

I have spoken with many faithful gay Orthodox Christians who have had various experiences within the Church. In some places, partnered homosexuals have been excommunicated, unless they repent of their relationship. In other places, and quite commonly, Orthodox priests have maintained a pretty effective "Don't Ask, Don't Tell" policy with regard to such communicants. Sometimes, however, Orthodox priests have even expressed support of faithful, monogamous, gay couples. I have spoken with Orthodox priests, bishops, and even published authors about this book and have been surprised by how much support I have found.

Ti tha pi o kosmos? "What will the world say?" This fear is what holds us back from exploring this issue. Too often a person's opinion on homosexuality is used as a cheap litmus test for how "conservative" or "liberal" one is, and the real issue is lost.

Too often the discussion around homosexuality in the Church focuses on sin, when the real question before us should be: *How can the Church faithfully minister to and love homosexual Orthodox Christians?* Jesus befriended those who were marginalized because he knew it was only in the security of loving, unconditional relationships that hearts and lives are healed. Similarly, we cannot explore the issue of homosexuality without hearing the life, stories, and witness of faithful, Orthodox Christians who happen to be gay.

It is my prayer that this anthology will open up dialogue and discussion within the Orthodox Church about the struggles, stories, and witness of lesbian, gay, bisexual, and transgender Orthodox Christians, and those who love them. May we hear their cries, and open our hearts to their needs.

January, 2010 —*Justin R. Cannon*

HELENA
GREEK ORTHODOX

I am the mother of a gay son. I am a convert to Orthodoxy largely due to my son's sharing of his newfound Christianity after he himself had converted to the Eastern Orthodox faith. He was able to answer every question and concern about the Orthodox faith. He took up his studies of Orthodoxy with the same fervor he had as a child for learning the Bible and studying Protestant theology.

My only son was my firstborn child. He was a beautiful baby and grew to be such a handsome little boy. As a baby of nine or ten months he always wanted my aunt, who visited often, to put her earrings on his ears. If they were clip on earrings she would put them on his ears and he would be very pleased.

He had twin sisters who were born when he was two. He had a hard time adjusting to the two of them because it meant I had little time then to spend exclusively with him reading to him, etc. Reading to him was something he loved and I had done a lot of reading to him before the twins were born. He once said that he loved his "sissies" but wished we could send them back where they came from.

When I was eight years old my mother had converted to the Protestant faith. I was at the time preparing for my first communion. Both sides of our family were Roman Catholic and there was much disapproval about her conversion and, consequently, mine. My son was very precocious regarding spiritual teachings. At that time we were very much involved in a Pentecostal protestant church. When he was three years old he asked our visiting pastor to explain the Trinity to him. He was very sincere when he asked for an explanation. This deep interest in spirituality and theology continued on as he grew.

I can't remember how old he was when he came to me with a question. I believe he may have been ten or eleven years old. His question was something like, "What do you think about the story of Sodom and Gomorrah in the Old Testament?" I was a bit taken back by his question, but gave him the usual explanation as I had heard it explained all of my adult life. How God was displeased with the actions of the men of Sodom and Gomorrah because they wanted to have sex with the angels that visited the city. Little did I know at that time, there was a terrible conflict torturing my young son.

As my son got into his teen years, I noticed him withdrawing from life. He would spend every day, for most of the day when he was home from school, shut away in his bedroom with the drapes drawn. When I would knock and go into his room, he would always be reading his Bible.

I would encourage him to go outside and play. He was not interested in the usual things most boys his age seemed to be interested in. He did like growing plants from seeds he had planted and tried to please me by attempting to occasionally come out of his room. He spent many hours playing the harmonica first and then the organ in our home. Later we got a piano and he took to that also. He could play any gospel song that he heard from memory.

He also spent time trying to learn Spanish. My mother was born in Spain. The family spoke Castilian Spanish and my son spent a lot of time learning Spanish with help from my aunt and a little help from my mother.

As the years passed, I became more and more concerned about his seclusion in his room. He did like to visit his grandparents who lived behind us. My mother, his grandmother, was very much into her Pentecostal beliefs and my son loved to ask her question after question regarding her beliefs.

I finally voiced my concern about our son to my husband. I wondered if our son could benefit from counseling. My husband was a professing Christian, on the deacon board, a Sunday school teacher, etc., but was an angry person who expressed his anger verbally and sometimes by throwing things or getting abusive. Other times he was cold and emotionally withdrawn. He told me there was nothing wrong with his son. As I knew there was nothing I could say that would convince him, I did not pursue the conversation any further with him. My concern, however, continued to escalate.

When my son was, I believe, seventeen years of age, he told me one Sunday night after church that he wanted to talk to me. His father was working that night and we had privacy. He opened up his heart to me because he knew how much I loved him and he felt safe to share his heart. The Baptist church where we were members at the time had a wonderful pastor and he had preached a sermon that night using, in part, the scripture reference from Romans 1. My son told me he was attracted to guys and had been ever since he could remember, back at least to the age of three. I was completely devastated by his news. It explained to me why he had spent most of his teen years praying and reading his Bible. He was praying for deliverance from this terrible torture that tore at the fiber of his soul. I did not know what to say. I was in such shock that I really do not know what I said to him. I am sure that I voiced concern for his soul, but I knew that this was not something that my son had chosen. All I knew was that I loved him and my heart was broken because of his intense suffering over this "problem." We were up most of the night talking and I felt like my life would never be the same again. I wanted to fix this terrible pain that my son was living through. Isn't that one of the things that mothers try to do for their children if possible—fix whatever the problem is to take away the pain?

I cannot even begin to put into words the pain I experienced and the many tears that I shed in the years that followed. I prayed over and over that God would deliver my son. I am sure God had already heard this prayer many times over from my son. I wondered what kind of a God would allow a child to suffer this kind of pain and then send him to hell for something that he wanted more than anything to be taken from him. He wanted to be attracted to a girl, get married, and have children.

I kept this very painful secret for many years, finally sharing it with one of my twin girls who said that she had known her brother was gay from the time she was young. She was sympathetic towards him and loved him.

My husband and I divorced a few years after I learned my son was gay. According to my son, his father has been able to accept the fact that his son is gay.

Over the years I have gradually come to accept completely the fact that my son is gay, even though I wish I could have seen him happily married and could have had grandchildren from him. I definitely do not believe that people who are gay should force themselves to marry to keep up appearances. That is a recipe for disaster for both parties in the marriage. I have accepted the fact that I know to be true, that he did not choose to be gay. I believe people who are gay were created by God. I have found them to be very gifted people. My heart goes out to the many children who have had parents, family and the church reject them because they are gay. I know that many gay people have been unable to bear the pain of rejection and have either submersed themselves in the drug culture, are alcoholics, or have ended up in prison, and I am sure many others have committed suicide. I believe that God loves them. He is the judge and he does not condemn love. Love is not to be confused with lust and hurting another human.

I pray that someday those in my family and the churches who have shown disgust, hatred, and rejection will realize that God is the merciful judge, not us. Surely the God of love is a just God. I sometimes wish these people had taken the time to sit down and have a heart-to-heart discussion with someone who is gay so they could understand that gay people are no different in loving another person than heterosexual people are. They should not say they don't know whether a person chooses to be gay unless they have engaged in a deep conversation with one who is gay. I believe no person would choose to be gay and therefore be hated and reviled as evil by their fellow human beings.

BARRY
RUSSIAN ORTHODOX

I cannot now remember any specific moment that I decided to become Orthodox, rather it seemed that the idea developed gradually over a period of three years; as if the prospect of such an undertaking somehow grew in potential until it reached a critical point where after the only obvious conclusion would have to be becoming a catechumen.

I always knew that it was an absurd thing to aspire to: a middle-aged gay Buddhist, in a long term relationship developing an interest in Orthodox Christianity, and particularly in Russian Orthodoxy, a Church noted for being especially homophobic. Many times over the last few years friends have asked "Why?" "It's an interest," I would reply. "Some people collect stamps, some play bowls, I study Orthodoxy." If only it were that simple. As I studied I gradually became utterly beguiled by its dogma, its liturgy and its sacraments, indeed by its utter other worldliness– even to such a degree that I was willing to forgive (and forget) the great harm committed by this institution to all those it considered, let's say, beyond the pale, in order to maintain its own integrity and position. Why did I do it? Why did I ever even begin to think that for me the church would turn a blind eye to my 'adopted lifestyle' and say, "It's ok Barry, at least your heart is in the right place," or words to that effect? Some degree of pride and arrogance played its part. There was a part of me that was going to be quietly pleased, and more than a little amused at being accepted into Orthodoxy, despite who or what I am. At no point did I consider not informing the priest of my, so called, 'life-style' but likewise I was never going to go sashaying into Vespers wearing fine stiletto's and singing the Trisagion in a quavering falsetto. The idea was to bide my time, do as the priest requested, and take the opportunity to disclose to him at the point that seemed most appropriate. That time came sooner than I thought and with consequences I had not foreseen.

I do not think that it actually crossed anyone's minds at the church that I may in fact be gay. It appeared that I would be received with open arms. The priest indicated that a lengthy catechesis would not be necessary in my case, and that the three sacraments of catechism, baptism, and chrismation could all be performed at the same time; that is, after a few informal meetings, in around two or three months time. I was so pleased and felt elated at the prospect of actually becoming Orthodox and participating in the life of the Church. For over the years of studying Orthodoxy it had began to dawn on me that it could never be understood from the outside as it were; that is its truths are not so much theoretical but practical, and that rather than being ascribed to, they are lived. I had come to consider that it was less an intellectual appreciation of some theological finery, rather a life that embraced a living liturgy and sacrament – Orthodoxy is not so much believed as done. And it had become something that I wanted to do.

This is not ancient history for me. All this has occurred only in the last few months, and I am only now very slowly starting to find my feet again after the events I am about to describe. Indeed the reason for writing this piece was not so much for others, as my story will hardly be unique, but as therapy for me: to tell myself the story and perhaps in some way find a form of resolution or at least a way forward. I needed to share this and had no one else with whom to share it. And to tell it accurately I probably need to spend at least a little time reflecting on my need to believe in the first place.

I have not needed a faith of any sort over that last few decades, for me Buddhism was a philosophy that I had accepted as being a rationale to live by. It was only when I started looking into Buddhism as a religion as opposed to a philosophy that it started to fall apart and I began to loose any interest in it.

I can honestly say that I have no real sense or awareness of the presence of a god. I choose to believe in a god, not because I am convinced that there is one, but rather because I consider life to be more reasonable, to take on a greater sense of purpose and meaning with such a belief. Creeds and dogma inform me of this chosen conviction, but the essence of which has so far eluded me. It is much like in the same way that a book of geography may inform me of a far distant land, to which I could, perhaps, at a future date venture. Being thus informed I accept that this place does indeed exist and that it only waits for me to embark on a voyage of discovery to visit those far off shores. Until then though, for now, the existence of God is limited to the acceptance of creed and dogma, written and perpetrated by those who have discovered and traveled to this far distant kingdom for themselves, often at great personal cost and sacrifice.

I am, it is fair to say though, at a complete loss to know just why it is I am so attracted to Orthodoxy. No doubt it is for many reasons, some of which I have already mentioned. There is that part of me that says flee from all forms of dogma, that such things are toxic to the soul; and yet, there is also that part of me that I recognize as grasping for dogma as one would a glass of water in a barren and parched wilderness. That here, within these ancient creeds, there is an oasis in the crying despair of the maw of this life. It is as if calling from the depths of Orthodoxy there is a voice that says, "Herein lies truth. When all else is fallible and failed, here on this rock, is the refuge for one's soul." I recognize a need for certainty and hope in a world so bereft of either attribute. Why is this? Some latent childhood guilt, a craving to return to the certainty of youth when ones father was always present to protect and to provide? How would I know if it was? I lack any such insight. I want so much for it all to be true (Orthodoxy that is) but how would I know? Why is all this so important? I lack answers, but it seems to me that Orthodoxy comes some way to addressing some of these questions. That is, in its liturgy and sacramental life the answers may not so much be found, but rather addressed in such a way that they are assuaged, and situated in such a way that the great mystery of all is acknowledged as one is led into the far greater mystery of the incarnation.

Leading up to my baptism/chrismation the priest and I had a couple of meetings where we talked of the history of the Church and the practicalities of an orthodox lifestyle. Theology was not an issue for me; it was more to do with icons and candles and prosphora, and the practical aspects of Orthodox life and sacrament. It was only when the priest came to visit me in my home that we reached the unbridgeable chasm. "You have a nice place here," the priest said as he came into the lounge. "Yes, Tony and I are very happy here." There was an awkward silence. "Who's Tony?" "My boyfriend, I'm gay." Another silence. "Barry why did you not tell me this before? I thought that you were single." "Well," I said, "It's only really the third time we've met for any practical conversation, and to be honest we talked of other things." "How long have you been together?" "Some twelve years now, why?" "You cannot be living in sin and be Orthodox. In fact, I cannot even consider you as a possible catechumen at this time; you really should not be taking part in any of the sacraments of the Church at all. You are either single and celibate or married; anything else is totally unacceptable in the Church. I'm sorry, but I had no idea." Over tea we talked for some twenty or thirty minutes. It was clear that we both felt uncomfortable with the situation. I was in a state of shock. "It's going to take me a long time to think this through," I said, "many months probably." After a short while he made his excuses and left. I had to get ready for work, but I felt sick to the core. I was, as we used to say, totally gutted.

I'm not a very quick or a particularly bright person, but I know that I could have confronted the priests homophobia there and then, and have demanded reasons, rationales and explanations, but why? By his own admission, the inexperienced priest was as uncomfortable as I was distressed, and putting him on the spot would have achieved nothing other than to embarrass him, or worse. And at the end of the day he is a priest, which is something I respect. But is it too much to expect a little respect in return? Who knows?

Up until this point, I had been attending vigil or liturgy each week—usually both. I stopped going. I was astonished at the amount of anger welling up inside me toward the Church and its outmoded stance. I felt utterly betrayed and just could not bring myself to face anyone or anything. This was perhaps the most surprising thing for me. Over the last couple of years I had often thought through the scenario of being rejected by the Church, I always knew that this was a possibility. What I had not counted on was my emotional response to this rejection. I really had no idea that I had such an emotional investment in becoming Orthodox. What was most surprising here was not so much that I was rejected (it is Russian Orthodoxy after all), but that I felt so dreadful about it.

It has taken many months for the anger to subside a little, and I have been to only three Vigils since that day in July. Although coming to terms with these events a little, I am still very unsure about the future in regards to my practicing Orthodoxy or even remaining committed to any form of Christianity for that matter. Do I resent the Church for this? How can I, she is the Church, who am I to find fault in her, in her lack of compassion and her inequalities? I can only look upon and reflect upon my own sins, such as they are. Have I really not understood the message of the Gospel at all in all of this? Am I really so corrupted that for me black is white and vice-versa? Is life really as the church would have me believe; the happy, redeemed, righteous and straight in one corner and all others cast into the oblivion of the other? Was the church really intended to be just an organization for heterosexuals? I cannot see this. For me, Calvary means, if anything, the complete and utter acceptance of all (even of those I don't think deserve it). When I look upon the life-giving cross this is what I find – life – not rejection and confusion. One incarnation, one savior, and one hope of salvation and redemption. What does the Church think it is trying to preserve in maintaining this prejudice? If it's integrity and truth, surly these were compromised long, long ago.

The priest had mentioned that Orthodoxy was about preparing one's soul for death. I on the other hand, had seen it as a resource for life; as that beautiful little prayer states: "My hope is in the Father, my refuge is in the Son, my shelter is in the Holy Spirit, O Holy Trinity glory to Thee." Hope, refuge and shelter were images that resonated to the core of my being. I was coming to the Church because I sensed a great need to be there. It was not necessarily something I could explain, it was something that was experienced, like hunger.

I recognize that I ask too many questions. Perhaps this demonstrates my bewildered state of mind at this time. This is one of the reasons I've found these events so difficult, for I had found respite in the deep truths and mystery of the liturgy and vigil. The Church was the place I went to quiet the questioning and to let the beauty of the mystery in the richly textured liturgical language speak its healing balm deep into my soul. We have reached a contradiction an impasse – which for now will remain – but for how long I really cannot say.

MATTHEW
GREEK ORTHODOX

My path of struggle to reconcile spirituality and sexuality which eventually led me into the Orthodox Church, started in adolescence. The growing awareness of my homosexual bent, as a devout, 12-year-old, Trinitarian-Pentecostal boy, traumatized me. Despite my devotion to God throughout much of my childhood, the unthinkable was happening: I was becoming more and more perverse, finding myself attracted to guys rather than girls, masturbating with abominable, sexual fantasies, and moving closer and closer to a destiny of eternal damnation in *the lake which burneth with fire and brimstone.*

Each day, as a teenager, I would beg God to *remove this thorn in my flesh*, to cast out this demon of perverse abomination, and to stretch out His hand of healing and make me whole, normal, and heterosexual. I would spend hours each day, singing hymns to God as I played my accordion and prayed for His deliverance, but no deliverance came. The retelling of it sounds melodramatic, but the living of it was true torture. My hope that this was *simply a phase I'm going through* was dying with each passing day and, in place of my hope, descended a deep-settled and profound sense of despair. My mother would come home and find me in darkness with the shades drawn studying the Bible or playing the accordion.

Having read and studied the Bible from the age of six, I was well aware by age 12 that God condemns homosexuals to death. So, waking up to find that I myself, in my heart, was a Sodomite destroyed all sense of self-worth or value. I developed a kyphosis in my spine due to being hunched over, always carrying about the heavy burden of my evil desires. My mom, my grandma, and a nurse in our congregation expressed their concern, asking me what it was that was bothering me so much, but I was too ashamed to tell them.

I suffered alone for five years until age 17 when I could bear it no more and I finally told another human being what it was that was tormenting me. I told my mom, "I'm attracted to guys." My mom's response was one of a frantic, Pentecostal mother. She retrieved a bottle of oil from the kitchen and anointed me, praying for God to heal me of this terrible thing. Her prayer confirmed to me what I had known all along: I was an abominable wretch, worthy of damnation because, for some unknown reason, I wanted to fall in love with a guy and love him, rather than a girl. Since my expectation as a child had been to grow up and marry a woman and since I had always wanted to be normal, not abnormal, the obvious conclusion was that I must be twisted and perverse in my very nature. In the words of John Calvin, I was clearly "totally depraved."

For the next 17 years I would continue to fight against the demon of condemnation and despair over my sexual orientation. During those 17 years, I "fell into sin" two times: the first time, at age 19, I was in a homosexual relationship that lasted a month. The pain of that relationship ending, coupled with my sense of guilt and shame over it, led me to remain celibate for the next five years. At age 22, I decided, out of fear, not to follow through with my pre-med major and apply to medical school because it was during the AIDS crisis and one of my college professors had just said that a doctor could lose his practice if people found out he was gay because they would fear getting AIDS from him. Though I didn't plan to live a "homosexual lifestyle," I was afraid that people would find out about my homosexual experience at age 19 and since I had no intention of misusing a woman to cover up my orientation by marrying her, I took the words of my college professor as a prediction of my future should I pursue a medical career.

At age 24, I met my second boyfriend at a meeting for homosexual Christians seeking deliverance from their homosexuality and "fell into sin" the second time in that 17-year period. I began teaching high school in a small town during which time my boyfriend came to visit me. Apparently we were seen kissing by some of the townspeople and the next day it was all over town that I was gay. Right after that, my relationship, having lasted three months, ended with me contracting from my boyfriend a sexually-transmitted disease, which I interpreted to be chastisement from God and a warning to me to *go up out of Sodom and not to turn back*. The remainder of that school year was a living hell for me due to the disrespect from students and their parents and the lack of support from the school administration. I decided not to pursue any legal action against them since I did not want to identify publicly as "gay." Instead, I went back into a ten-year closet where I attempted through prayer, fasting, and bible study to overcome my homosexuality and become heterosexual– *the way God intended*.

Refusing to subject myself to further abuse in the public school environment and not knowing what else to do with my life, I decided to pursue my life-long interest in theology. During my first year of seminary I became more aware of the distinct history and theology of the Orthodox Church. Then, during my second year, I met an Orthodox Christian who invited me to a Divine Liturgy. The liturgy with its repetitiousness, its lack of musical instruments, and its less concise structure when compared with the Roman Catholic liturgy did not compel me to come back. What did compel me to return, however, was the theology found in the prayers, preaching, icons, and the sense of its continuity throughout history.

After several months of intense study and hours of discourse with the parish priest, I was received into the Orthodox Church. During my first confession, when I confessed my *homosexuality*, I was shocked when the priest seemed more concerned about other things I had mentioned and made no reference to my homosexual orientation. Later, in another confession, he encouraged me to quit focusing on my homosexuality and begin focusing on such sins as greed, envy, slander, laziness, gluttony, hatred, etc. When I left that confession, I felt like a new man. I began to realize that my adverse obsession with my homosexuality had been suspending my spiritual growth by keeping me focused off of problems in my life which I could actually change.

I had entered the Orthodox Church with the hope of defeating my homosexuality, becoming heterosexual, getting married, and possibly even becoming a priest. During the next seven years, my spiritual father discouraged me from pursuing the priesthood given my sexual orientation, although I had not had sex with a man for over ten years. I began psychotherapy in hopes of changing my orientation, but that didn't seem to be happening. During that time, I quit focusing so much on my homosexuality and began focusing more on the basic sins mentioned by my spiritual father. I began learning about the Orthodox concepts of *akríbeia* vs. *oikonomía* which seem to parallel the concepts of *law* vs. *grace, the letter of the law* vs. *the spirit of the law, the tablets of stone* vs. *the fleshly tablets of the heart, the law of bondage* vs. *the law of liberty,* and *the Torah of the Old Covenant* vs. *the Royal Law of Love of the New Covenant.* I began experiencing the liberating Orthodox focus on existential living in communion with God instead of my previous, Western-Christian obsession with the rules and regulations of an external law. I learned that the limiting of the number of sacramental mysteries to "seven" is a western concept and that another ancient and long-celebrated mystery of the Orthodox Church, like the anointing of kings, is the mystery of *Adelphopoiesis* which, like marriage, is a sanctification of a non-Christian rite, in this case, that of the same-sex union of blood-brotherhood, sealed not with the co-mingling of corrupt, human blood as in the pagan rite, but rather sealed by a sharing in the incorruptible blood of Christ with a private exchange of baptismal crosses or some other private token as a sign of this brotherhood. In addition, I learned that the Church Fathers were human, made mistakes, had no claim to papal infallibility, and said things, at times, that could well be labeled anti-semitic, anti-scientific, and misogynistic. I also learned that the scripture verses used to condemn homosexual love were not so clear-cut in their meaning as many would have us believe.

As an Orthodox Christian, I was beginning to see the world in living color, not in the black and white rigidity of Western legalism and Thomas Aquinas' naturalism, but in the freedom of life lived under the direction of the Spirit of Love against which there is no law. Even so, despite this growing awareness, I had not yet accepted my sexual orientation as a viable way of living under the Law of Love. Instead, I had to pass through a traumatic experience in order to cast from myself, like the myrrh-bearing women, an inherited condemnation. The trauma of being drugged and raped by someone I trusted and loved shattered my world in many ways, but throughout the aftermath of that terrible realization, my mainstay was the Orthodox Church. As I grappled with the horror of what had happened to me, I came face to face with a huge distinction that must be drawn between various expressions of sexuality in order to preserve the beauty of love as uncorrupted by the ugliness of humiliating subjugation and enslavement.

Like the men of Sodom sought to do to the angels, the man who drugged and raped me committed an act, not of love, but of humiliating subjugation and enslavement. Love has nothing to do with such an act. In realizing what this man had done to me, I realized that the way he related to me was of a different nature than the way I wished to relate to another man with whom I was in love. My desire as a homosexual man is to fall in love with another man who likewise is in love with me, and to express my love for him, to him, on every level, including erotic and sexual expression, not forcing him like a rapist, but pleasing him according to his own desires in a way which is also pleasing to me. When I realized this distinction first hand, one of my initial reactions was to get angry at people who compare the rapists of Sodom to a man such as myself in order to condemn me in my desire to love another homosexual man who is in love with me.

Love is an amazing and unpredictable thing. Sometimes love saves life and other times love kills. Love sometimes moves beyond the boundaries of what is considered normal, decent, or upstanding. Sometimes love doesn't look like what we would expect love to look like. But love, in any relationship, is always patient, kind, generous, humble, decent, unselfish, even-tempered, non-judgmental, respectful, truth-loving, faithful, hopeful, enduring, unfailing. Since this kind of love can exist in any relationship, I could no longer see any reason why I could not love another man on every level of my being. Strangely, I thank God that He allowed me to be drugged and raped because that ordeal brought me a new and happy clarity of vision regarding my own desire to love and share my life with another man.

I felt liberated with my new realization of the perfect law of freedom, the law of love, which makes *all things permissible*, but requires discretion on the part of the lover lest he be dominated by something other than love. For the first time in my life I began actively searching for a life partner among the gay community. I searched for three years and was extremely frustrated by the immaturity, alcoholism, addictions, promiscuity, untrustworthiness, irreverence, and other undesirable traits which I found in the men I dated. I wanted to find a nice, gay, Orthodox Christian guy, but wasn't finding anyone with whom I wished to share my life. In an act of desperation, I threw erotic love aside and settled on being with an admirable man with whom I was not in love. I felt safe with him and, following the rape, a sense of safety was, perhaps, my one and only requirement for a relationship.

At the onset of this new, unfulfilling relationship, I sought to find an Orthodox Church where my partner, an Anglican, and I could attend with a sense of safety. I was no longer living where my first parish was and so we attended an Antiochian church for a while until we realized that the priest there was a convert from an Evangelical, Protestant background. Consequently, my partner and I both made the assumption that this priest would not be "gay-friendly" and that we probably wouldn't find any "gay-friendly" Orthodox priests so we began seeking alternatives. The alternative we found was a non-canonical "Orthodox" church under an acclaimed, old-calendar bishop who was no longer in communion with the bishops of his previous jurisdiction. I remained with this non-canonical group for almost five years, working to make this struggling group succeed, being driven by my own worry of losing this last thread of the "church" which I thought was available to me as a gay man. During those five years, I became quite angry with the Orthodox clergy because I believed they would withhold from me the Body and Blood of Christ because I was "living in sin" with my gay partner (despite the fact that we weren't even sexually involved). The Gospel stories of the Syrophoenician woman and of the woman with the issue of blood seemed to be pushing me to make contact and persevere with the clergy of the canonical Orthodox Church. I wanted to hound the clergy like a dog begging crumbs from the table, but I was afraid. I knew that the same Torah which condemned *man-lying-with-man* was also used by some Orthodox to prohibit menstruating women from approaching the Holy Chalice. That fact gave me further impetus to beg, despite what any law might say. I was willing to call myself a dog—a word used in the Old Testament for male, pagan, temple-prostitutes—in a plea for some priest to have mercy on me and give me access to the Divine Mysteries of Christ, but I was so afraid of rejection.

Finally, I got past the fear and I went and spoke with a priest. He did not, *per se*, condone my homosexuality, but neither did he condemn me, or prohibit me from approaching the Chalice. I felt supported by him to continue to *work out my own salvation with fear and trembling*. His approach was quite in line with the concept of *oikonomia* which I had read about. And, although he had the authority to apply the harsh strictness of *akribeia* in line with the current Orthodox understanding of my issues, he was gracious and did not do so. I also spoke with another younger priest about this issue and he told me that, in the same way that he would not allow a thief who was currently stealing to approach the Chalice, he would not allow me, a practicing homosexual, to do so. When I calmly questioned his comparison of homosexuality with thievery, he became indignant, reminiscent of the anger with which Christ drove the money-changers out of the Temple, and said, "This is *my* house!" (referring to the Church), "and when you're in *my* house, you'll do as I say!" At that point, I decided not to argue with him and to go back to the other priest I had spoken to.

So I quit attending the non-canonical group and began attending a Greek Orthodox Church. A year later, my partner, chose to go beyond our unfulfilling relationship and we broke up. I have met several other gay people at the Church and have "come out" to some of the non-gay parishioners, though I am selective about whom I "come out" to. There is always a fear that some priest or bishop is going to "crack down" and perform a witch hunt and drive me and other gay people out of the Church, as I know has occurred in the past in some parishes. The parish priest, though, assures me that no priest or bishop has that kind of authority because they themselves are sinners just like the rest of us. I guess my fear, rational or irrational as it may be, is that *nothing can separate us from the love of God in Christ Jesus our Lord* except one of the clergy.

I know for a fact that not all Orthodox Christians reject homosexuals as viable expressions of our common humanity. I also know that many of those for whom we pray that they *may rightly explain the word of truth* may also be self-loathing homosexuals who would have a most difficult time allowing anyone else to embrace themselves as persons created in the image of God and free to love according to nature or beyond nature, especially those persons whom God has allowed through genetic anomaly or other means to be saliently unique in their expression of our common humanity, transcending the categories of gender/sexual normalcy.

ELIZABETH
EASTERN ORTHODOX

I must have been somewhere around two or three years old when I realized there was something about me that was different in terms of sex and gender. At that age, of course, I had no idea that boys and girls differed in terms of morphology and genetics, but it was plain to me that there were differences in play and social interactions. What began for me was an uncomfortable realization that my parents understood me to be a boy, while I somehow vaguely understood myself to be a girl. What followed were years of secrecy, observation, analysis, and efforts to "blend in" as unobtrusively as possible with boys. Pretty much a loner, I kept people at a distance. For me, fear was constant: fear that I would be found out, unmasked, reprimanded, and punished; fear of males and masculinity; fear of failure; fear of intimacy of any kind. My masculine presentation was generally effective, but there were times when I felt like "a stranger in a strange land."

In high school and college, though I was attracted to women and managed pretty much to act the role of a "straight guy," I just wasn't able to understand or negotiate the complexity of boy-girl relations, and so I opted to avoid dating situations. In college, I ran across a couple of books, one by Christine Jorgensen and the other by Jan Morris, and suddenly with that new knowledge of transsexualism, half of my questions seemed to have answers. Gender identity was something separate from physical morphology; biology is not destiny: the shape of my skin did not necessarily determine my sense of self. On the other hand, what remained was my attraction for women, and I struggled without success with the question of how I might be a transsexual and a lesbian. It seemed an impossible situation, and I couldn't wrap my mind around it, and so in the end, I nudged the issue of gender identity to one side. By a miracle I overcame my self-defense mechanism of isolation, and entered into a relationship with a fine woman, and we were married. Confusion, conflicts, and fear remained, but we were both focused on our jobs, a mortgage, little league, and Cub Scouts. So, it was not until I was in my thirties that I was finally willing to give some attention to the core issues of gender identity and sexual orientation. Part of 'coming to terms with it' had to do with a kind of reconciliation with my emerging identity as an Orthodox Christian.

My family was Roman Catholic, and I attended the local Roman church and Catholic schools up through high school, college, and graduate school. Like many college-aged people in the sixties and seventies, by the time I finished college I had pretty much lost touch with organized religion. A few years later, though, by the time I was married with a five-year-old, it seemed like a good time to get re-connected with some faith community. We thought it might be good, too, for us all to have the experience of Sunday school, weekly worship, fish fries, and spaghetti dinners. Our marriage continued to flounder, but I occupied myself with graduate school and reading. In retrospect, it occurs to me that it was undernourished, and that was partly because of my continuing "issues" with intimacy. After a few years with the Episcopal Church, I began to feel dissatisfied with that tradition, and eventually left my spouse and son there while I found my way to a local Orthodox parish. At about the same time, I found myself wondering what to do about my emerging sense of being a still closeted transsexual in the Orthodox Church, and for that matter, still attracted to women. Like many recent converts to Orthodoxy, I was enthusiastic, exuberant, and (still am, I suppose) a bit overeager to "get it right," not just with Orthodoxy, but with sexual orientation and gender identity. For me, it developed into a kind of "don't ask, don't tell" situation. While it may have been fairly clear to some folks that I was not your traditional run-of-the-mill married heterosexual parent, it never seemed like there was something to discuss, or for that matter, anybody to engage in that sort of discussion.

By the mid-90s, our marriage was concluded, and I was divorced and celibate. I had also transitioned fairly successfully from male to female, as well as from "straight" to "lesbian," and I was alone, hundreds of miles from my son and his mother. Still, I wondered what would happen if I were in a relationship. For that time, though, I was glad to be in church working out my relationship with God, and even began wondering if (and for that matter, how!) I should give thought to entering monastic life.

When I moved to New York, I encountered people who attended Dignity and Integrity, and for quite a while I chose to attend, not only an Orthodox parish (generally for Vespers), but more often an Anglo-Catholic one with a quite a few LGBT folks. After a short while, too, I found my way to the local Axios community, a fellowship for LGBT Eastern and Orthodox Christians, which met at the local LGBT Community Center once a month for Vespers and discussion (*See* "A Brief History" on page 79). It was interesting and exciting to find a network of support and encouragement and a place where the conversation can affirm an individual's sexual orientation and gender identity within a context of Orthodox faith and tradition. Here were people who had read John Boswell and Virginia Mollenkott, where dialogue was possible with respect to the marriage of LGBT people and the ordination of women. Here too were people who attended churches all over the city, people I might encounter on a Sunday morning, those who loved the Orthodox Church and who encountered and struggled with prejudice, homophobia, and transphobia in their parish communities.

As I began to flex my spiritual muscles, I began reading books by Elisabeth Behr-Sigel, Virginia Mollenkott, and others. I continued to grow in my identity as a Christian Orthodox transsexual lesbian woman and as a member of the LGBT community, and as such re-examined those "clobber passages" from Holy Scriptures that are so often used to isolate, frighten, demean and dismiss us. Conversations with other LGBT Christians enabled me to see myself as a beloved, affirmed child of God, no longer alienated and isolated, but part of a community and heir to a tradition.

Eventually, just a bit more than ten years ago, once I began to develop some computer and internet literacy, I found that there are some seemingly "unorthodox" faith communities that identify as Orthodox, but are openly hospitable to the LGBT community. Admittedly, these are non-canonical, but some of them have a strong commitment to the Orthodox faith, witness, and tradition, to the social and societal implications of Matthew's chapter 25, and to a kind of radical hospitality, to diversity, and to LGBT inclusion. Here, "there can be neither Jew nor Greek, neither slave nor free, neither male nor female…for all are one in Christ Jesus" (Gal 3: 28-29). With reference to issues of sexual identity, it has been good for me to engage is what might be considered "ecumenical dialogue" with self-described "queer theologians" and feminist theologians. The results of that dialogue, entered with such hesitation and misgivings, have been so rewarding. Fairly secure in my Orthodox faith, family, and community, I am glad to have met and formed respectful and productive friendships with these

Christians from other traditions. In addition, for close to nine years now, I've been blessed to be in a wonderful, loving, holy relationship with another woman. Now, as never before, and here, as nowhere else, I have felt a sense of secure welcome and full acceptance.

Although the journey for the most part has been productive and affirming, it is very sad that much of it has taken me away from "canonical" Orthodoxy, and that old sense of isolation, exclusion, separation, and "otherness" often returns to nag me, to call into question the decisions I have made. Part of the problem is bioethics and sociology. We Orthodox, in the pre-conciliar meetings that occur from time to time in preparation for a Great Council, need to find more effective ways to reconcile faith and science. We need to re-examine our traditions and our Canon Law in light of modern culture, science, psychology, and medicine: particularly psychiatry and endocrinology. We need to re-examine and re-evaluate our understanding of the sacraments, of family, and of vocation. We need to understand and appreciate the reality that diversity exists, and is of God. We need to re-visit our anthropology, not in order to surrender to postmodernism or secular humanism, but rather to see God as the first iconographer, and all people in all their diversity – physical, spiritual, sexual, intellectual – as images of God and of God's immense, relentless love. We need to find ways to welcome all of God's children.

BISHOP PAUL PETER JESEP
LGBTS CHRISTIAN WITNESS IS PART OF ORTHODOXY

"God will always have something more to teach man," counsels St. Irenaeus of Lyons, "and man will always have something more to learn from God."[i] So it can be said of many Orthodox Christians regarding their misunderstanding of the Creator's lesbian, gay, bisexual, transgender, and searching (LGBTS) children.

Orthodox Christian leaders have focused much time and energy on homosexuality. Genuine dialogue is needed where one side listens to the other. There cannot be a true Orthodox witness without the LGBTS community.

Confusion over homosexuality by parts of the religious community has limited or prevented Christian engagement. The Giver of Light calls us to leave places of personal spiritual safety. Institutional Orthodoxy[ii] is called to do so as well.

All sides of this contentious issue must find the Holy Author in stillness. The distance that now exists prevents community. This limits the Holy Spirit from bringing the faithful to greater fullness as one family with the same Creator, in which some members are created differently.

At every stage of religious development spiritual leaders criticized social change. As time moved on it modified its views toward serfdom, absolute autocracy, complacency toward anti-Semitism, and denying women the right to vote, among other things. What is Orthodoxy? Hopefully, "orthodox" love.

The Orthodox Church sometimes is still reacting to the Age of Enlightenment that laid the foundations for the French and Russian Revolutions. These revolutions were not just popular uprisings of the people and great thinkers against inept, unjust monarchies that abused and exploited their subjects. They were also revolutions against corrupt, relativist clericalism with a secular focus that provided royalty with moral legitimacy.

Although the Age of Enlightenment took clear aim at faith, not all of its supporters thought belief in the Almighty merited criticism. As discussed later, Hryhorij Savyc Skovoroda (1722-1794), a Ukrainian Orthodox Christian and a product of the Enlightenment, balanced faith and science without being scholastic. As a compatibilist he believed humankind's free will was not contrary to God's intent or authority.

Orthodoxy is not just a doctrine. It is mysticism, spiritual wellbeing, and living in the fullness of God that is not scholastic, but reflective of a deep spirituality. One Orthodox theological outline is offered here to understand, heal wounds, better communicate, and bring people together to find, in the words of philosopher Vladimir Solovyov (1853-1900), "a unifying and organizing principle of humanity" where religion moves beyond "insolvency" to "a more positive and all-embracing one."[iii]

The spiritual experience of the LGBTS community is already part of the Church. It just hasn't been acknowledged and embraced yet. Solid Orthodox theology and ethics, a subset of the greater body of Church teachings, can faithfully include these loved and valued children of God as equal, respected members of the family.

PREVAILING ATTITUDES

OLD WORLD ORTHODOXY

Negative views toward homosexuality are relatively consistent throughout the Orthodox world with the clear exception of the canonically recognized Finnish Orthodox Church.[iv] Condemnation of God's LGBTS children stems from several factors: fear, culture, ignorance, misreading scripture, negative stereotypes, perceived threats to religious teachings, and a belief that it's an unnatural lifestyle choice.

In 2003, the Russian Orthodox hierarchy had the Chapel of the Vladimir Icon of the Mother of God in Nizhny Novgorod leveled after Fr. Vladimir Enert, now defrocked "for blasphemy against the sacrament of marriage," solemnized the union of Denis Goglyev and Mikhail Morozev.[v]

Mr. Goglyev denounced the Church for becoming "a depraved institution, practically a sect. It spits on its own canons. Only Lenin and Stalin destroyed churches."[vi] He suggested that the Church leadership has moved away from God's love to a form of clericalism thinly veiled in the Body of Christ.

In addition, the decision to level the church implies that a legitimate solemnization did occur since it was conducted by a priest. Otherwise the priest could have been quietly defrocked and the matter ignored. Instead, the extreme reaction received international attention raising the question of why this shook Russian Orthodoxy to its core.

Several years ago Patriarch Alexy II, leader of the Russian Orthodox Church and a known collaborator of the Soviet secret police[vii], told the Parliamentary Assembly of the Council of Europe, a human rights advocacy group, that the continent must not abandon its Christian values for moral relativism. To do so would be a "break between human rights and morality." This break "threatens the European civilization."[viii]

He told the gathering that a "new generation of rights" contradicts "morality, and in how human rights are used to justify immoral behavior." He especially focused on homosexuality. The Patriarch called it "an illness" and a "distortion of the human personality like kleptomania." In objecting to a planned gay rights parade in Moscow he asked, "Why don't we have advertising for kleptomania?"[ix]

The Russian Orthodox Church rejects "Western" human rights. Although historically, scientifically, and sociologically inaccurate[x] and despite scandals within Orthodoxy[xi], the Moscow Patriarchate

47

has consistently blamed the West for homosexual activity that allegedly contributes to Europe's systematic moral and secular decline that has crept into the former Soviet Union.

Homosexuality is viewed as an affront to both the Church and an infliction on the individual. The Church, as spiritual doctor, must soteriologically treat and cure the disease. The Moscow Patriarchate has expressed strong reservations toward the Universal Declaration of Human Rights as adopted by the United Nations in 1949. In 2006, the 10th World Council of Russian People, an advocate for Russian Orthodoxy and a type of messianic mission for Holy Russia issued its own declaration noting that "freedom of choice leads to self-destruction and damages human dignity." "Religious tradition" should be determinative of "good" and "evil."[xii]

Collectively and individually, all Christian leaders, regardless of denomination, must be careful not to become like the Grand Inquisitor as described in Dostoevsky's *Brother's Karamazov*. Although widely interpreted as an assault on the Roman Catholic hierarchy, it has at least one message for the Orthodox as well – do not replace Christ with the flawed thinking of man. Jesus returns to earth and is confronted by the Inquisitor. The Inquisitor lecturers Jesus about his idealism noting that humankind is better off guided by a church that makes decisions for it removing the heavy responsibilities of freedom.[xiii]

In 2009, the City of Moscow banned a gay rights parade. Mayor Yuri Luzhkov, who once referred to the LGBTS community as a "satanic act," said through his spokesperson, Sergei Tsoi that "not only do they destroy morals within our society, but they consciously provoke disorder..."[xiv] On May 16, 2009, efforts to hold a parade without municipal authorization resulted in the arrest of forty demonstrators.[xv] Just a few years earlier Amnesty International issued a global report citing Russia for ignoring rising hate crimes against foreigners, immigrants, and sexual minorities.[xvi]

"In our judgment, homosexuality [is] a symptom of degeneracy which could destroy our race," is not an observation from the mayor or the Moscow Patriarchate, but one made about sixty years earlier by Heinrich Himmler.[xvii] Himmler was charged with carrying out Hitler's Final Solution for Jews, gypsies, gentile Slavs, political prisoners, gays and lesbians, the mentally ill, and the physically disabled.

In September 2009, comments made by the Orthodox Church Moscow Patriarchate in Ukraine against a celebrity brought renewed attention to discrimination that the LGBTS community endures. Although it was not the intent of this Orthodox branch, its public criticism again highlighted the need for open, honest discussion among the faithful regarding homosexuality.

Acclaimed singer and composer Sir Elton John and his husband, David Furnish, ran into a cultural and religious roadblock when they unofficially showed interest in adopting a fourteen month old HIV-positive boy from a Ukrainian orphanage where love is in want, healthcare is modest, facility conditions are primitive, and the chances that a child "with the gay disease" will be accepted into a family in a very homophobic society unlikely.

The church spokesperson offered the comments *after* the Ukrainian government issued a statement that prohibited the possibility of adoption due, in part, to the couple's respective ages, 62 and 47. The law does not allow adoption if the would-be parents are 45 or over.[xviii] The possibility, though remote, that the husbandless alcoholic mother would reclaim her child and that the Sir Elton's marriage would be recognized under Ukrainian civil law were additional obstacles.

The international story spotlighted several things.[xix] It showed ungratefulness for Sir Elton's work to treat and prevent AIDS in a country with Europe's fastest growing number of cases. The acclaimed singer-composer had traveled to Ukraine at the request of Olena Franchuk, founder of an AIDS organization and daughter of former Ukrainian president Leonid Kuchma.[xx]

Another issue spotlighted was the public homophobia by one of Ukraine's three branches of Orthodoxy. This is not to say that the other two or the Byzantine Catholic Church would disagree since the teachings on homosexuality are similar. The foreign-based Moscow Patriarchate in Ukraine, however, garnered the attention.

According to the Church's spokesperson, homosexuality "is a sin, it is against nature, and it represents the dead end of human development." LGBTS individuals "are people who succumb to their passions." The priest underscored that Sir Elton "is a sinner." There "is no other word for it."[xxi]

In Ukraine, there are petition drives to pressure the Verkhovna Rada, the country's parliament, to criminalize "propaganda of same-sex sexual relations."[xxii] In late 2005, a handful of academics from the Academy of Sciences of Ukraine signed a letter appealing to Ukrainian religions and provincial governments to protect the country against homosexuality, lesbianism, pedophilia, disgraceful phenomena, and same-sex marriage. They referred to homosexuality as immoral, a perversion, and the degradation of modern society. It only could be corrected by Christian psychiatry.[xxiii]

Interestingly, they called on priests, among others, who marry same-sex couples to repent, suggesting that the practice may be more widespread in Ukraine then one would think.[xxiv]

If an absence of sin were a prerequisite for those in a position of civil or religious trust, then there would be no popes, priests, patriarchs, lawyers, politicians, or heterosexual adoptive parents. In light of the ongoing population explosion human development is hardly heading for a "dead end."

Succumbing to passions isn't necessarily a bad thing since a heterosexual couple needs a little bit of it to help conceive a child. More important, intellectual honesty does not allow a group or the personhood of an individual to be defined by sex.[xxv] No healthy relationship – gay or straight – is grounded in physical passions.

A straight or homosexual relationship will fail if it is not grounded in love, honesty, friendship, communication, and mutual respect, among other things. Successful homosexual relationships, and there are many, have many similarities to successful heterosexual relationships.

Pope Shenouda, Patriarch of the Coptic Orthodox Church, told a gathering of his priests in England that homosexuality "ought not to be a matter of discussion" in the Church. It is "against nature." "Sexual expression," he said "is permitted only within marriage, between man and woman, male and female. Anything else is an abnormality."[xxvi]

He added that "Carnal persons cannot inherit the kingdom of heaven." The Pope reminded his audience that according to Hebrew Scriptures homosexuals were punished with death.[xxvii] The homosexual possesses a "debased mind" whose actions are "against the Mysteries of the Church."

The Pope reaffirmed the usual misinformation noting that homosexuality could be medically and spiritually cured. He added that God's judgment on Sodom proved the Creator's disdain for such behavior.[xxviii]

The use of "carnal" by some Christian leaders reflects an ongoing misunderstanding of homosexuality. Instead, the emphasis should be on the love, spiritual union, and emotional intimacy that can and does exist within same-sex relationships.

In 2009, the Serbian Orthodox Church described a planned gay rights march, later canceled, a "parade of shame."[xxix] Seventy-five percent of Romania's primarily Orthodox population trusts the Church. The Romanian Church accuses human rights groups of interfering with government policy. Civil government's reluctance to address discrimination against LGBTS citizens stems from the very real threat that elected officials will be excommunicated by the Church if they outlaw LGBTS discrimination.[xxx]

During a GayFest event in the Romanian capital of Bucharest the bishop called the event "an outrage to morality and to the

51

family."[xxxi] In Bulgaria, an Orthodox prelate referred to a planned gay rights parade as "the fruits of darkness."[xxxii]

"[A]ll kinds of homosexual relations are unnatural and worth condemning," according to a deacon speaking on behalf of the Armenian Araratian Patriarchal Diocese. Homosexuality "is considered a disgusting phenomenon and sin."[xxxiii] The views don't change much in nearby Belorussia where sexual minorities were denied an opportunity to show solidarity in a parade honoring the victims of the Chornobyl nuclear disaster.[xxxiv]

A 1990 statement issued by a joint commission of the Eastern and Oriental Orthodox churches provided that there must be co-operation that includes "as far as possible" instructing the faithful about "modern dangers" such as homosexuality.[xxxv]

At the Seventh Meeting of the Heads of the Oriental Orthodox Churches in the Middle East in 2004, the Common Declaration issued included a passage regarding suspension of dialogue with the Anglican Communion due to the consecration of gay Episcopal Bishop V. Gene Robinson. "Once again," the Declaration read, "we affirm our position that all practice and behavior related to marriage and sexual orientation must be in accord with the biblical and moral teachings of our Churches."

Theological dialogue would not resume until the Anglican Communion resolved this issue in a manner acceptable to Orthodox standards.[xxxvi] Even if the Oriental Orthodox Churches don't agree with the elevation of a gay Episcopal priest to bishop, suspension of formal dialogue distances Christians from one another. If sin is prevalent isn't it all the more reason to engage with the Anglican Communion?

ORTHODOXY IN THE AMERICAS

Homosexuality "has never been accepted as a normal behavior and people have never been open about it comfortably," according to a

Coptic Orthodox priest in Ohio. He calls it a life style choice and "objectively [a] grave evil and intrinsically disordered." He tells the faithful that homosexuals are "foolish, faithless, heartless and ruthless."[xxxvii]

The Ukrainian Orthodox Church of Canada takes a more gentle approach than its Coptic brethren making a distinction between orientation and an expression of one's sexuality. It affirms the dignity of gays and lesbians condemning the act, not the person.[xxxviii]

The Standing Conference of the Canonical Orthodox Bishops in the Americas (SCOBA) issued a statement that same-sex unions are not blessed or sanctioned by the Church. The "Sacrament of Marriage reflects the union between Christ and His Church…sexual relations between a husband and wife are to be cherished and protected as a sacred expression of their love…"

According to SCOBA, "The Orthodox Church cannot and will not bless same-sex unions…marriage…is a sacred institution ordained by God, homosexual union is not."[xxxix] It should be noted that any state in America that passes a law approving same sex marriage cannot require a church to bless such a union. It would violate the freedom of religion clauses of state and federal constitutions.

Similar to the Ukrainian Orthodox Church of Canada SCOBA says that "we must stress that persons with a homosexual orientation are to be cared for with the same mercy and love that is bestowed by our Lord Jesus Christ upon all of humanity."[xl]

In citing the Book of Acts, the Russian Orthodox Church Outside Russia (ROCOR), stated that "We must obey God rather than men" (5:29).[xli] In making this statement, however, it should also apply to popes, patriarchs, and bishops. History is filled with examples where Church leaders have made regrettable decisions that included: opposition to a woman's right to vote, punishing people who believed that the earth revolved around the sun, and supporting the divine right of kings regardless of the autocrat's administrative incompetence and abusiveness to his or her people.

FINNISH ORTHODOXY'S SPIRITUAL LEADERSHIP

The Finnish Orthodox Church, with origins dating back to the 12th century, is an autonomous archbishopric of the Patriarchate of Constantinople. It is an anomaly in the debate about the Almighty's LGBTS children in the Orthodox faith. Unlike other branches of Orthodoxy it has and continues to push the envelope on social, spiritual, and religious LGBTS issues without risking its canonical status with the Ecumenical Patriarch.

In May 2009, a Finnish Orthodox clergyman participated in the European Forum of Gay, Lesbian, Bisexual and Transgender Christian Groups held in Helsinki.[xlii] Adjunct Professor and theologian Vesa Hirvonen from the University of Helsinki also spoke. The professor posed the question, "Does homosexuality challenge the doctrine of the Church?" He answered with a resounding no since "homosexuality and question concerning sexual orientation do not challenge the faith of the Church, but they challenge its interpretation of love. They challenge the Church to preach and live love applied to the conditions of our time."[xliii]

Furthermore, the participation of the Finnish Orthodox clergyman at this forum showed the willingness to leave comfort zones while suggesting a strategic, incremental approach to acknowledge the ongoing Christian witness of the LGBTS community.

In a 2008 interview with the Finnish Orthodox publication *Aamun Koitto (The Morning Journal)*, His Eminence Archbishop Leo (Makkonen) said of Hannu Poyhonen's book condemning homosexuality that "Members of the clergy are educated, independent-minded…I am convinced that they are able to examine the records…[with] open eyes."

He added that the Finnish Orthodox Church "is careful not to take a strong stand on sexual ethics. It is because the current situation of Church unity can easily be compromised."

His Eminence made an observation all too often overlooked about the determined refusal to openly discuss homosexuality. "The fall of Communism," he noted has been a recent occurrence. "Eastern European churches still need time to embrace a culture of open debate."

In responding to a question about an Orthodox couple registering their same-sex relationship, the Archbishop observed that in "a democratic country, a functioning church [is required] to respect the rules of democracy. Legal registration of civil partnership[s] and blessing [by] a church are quite different. The Church blesses relationship[s] between man and woman. In practice, anyone belonging to a church would probably not be asked about family background as a condition for participation in church activities or services."[xliv]

This comment underscores the central problem with gay marriage today. Marriage has come to mean both a sacrament and a civil legality. The word is now interchanged to refer to blessings of a church and economic rights through civil marriage. This concern could be easily addressed by requiring any couple wanting to join together to obtain a government certificate of "civil union." If someone wants to be married they should find a priest to perform the service.

DOING ORTHODOX THEOLOGY

A primary reason for the strong, uncompromising reaction from Orthodox leaders to the LGBTS community may stem from how it does theology. It is different from the Western approach, which may be one of the reasons why Lutherans, Episcopalians, and the United Church of Christ, among others, have taken an inclusive approach to homosexuals.

In addition, a strong apostolic tradition of agreement among Western Protestant denominations does not exist. There is less urgency to speak with one voice since their respective faith traditions do not identify their denomination with such a need.

Orthodox churches are national in nature. Each country has one. Councils for the Eastern Church are as important today as they were many centuries ago.[xlv]

Declaring, as many Orthodox leaders have done, that the issue is settled and there will be no discussion on it other than its condemnation, does an extraordinary disservice to the faith. It is a missed opportunity for Christians on both sides of the issue to struggle in community to find common ground. It will not be an easy fellowship, but it will, nonetheless, be genuine.

The ministry of Jesus involved a new covenant. It challenged the norms of his day. Similarly, a handful of scriptural references that appear to condemn homosexuality must be revisited and we must remain open to different scholarly and theological interpretations.

Many Christians legitimately point out that Sodom and Gomorrah involved the potential for the violent crime of gang rape. The threatened violence, however, had nothing to do with a loving, monogamous, same sex union or relationship. In addition, the story of Sodom and Gomorrah is referenced elsewhere in scripture offering a clearer explanation as to why God destroyed the cities. The Maker of All Good did not have homosexuality in mind.

Isaiah laments that he lives "among a people of unclean lips" (Isaiah 6:5). Israel is likened to Sodom and Gomorrah for infidelity, irreverence, and false humility to God. There is no mention of or even reference to sexual immorality (1:10). Specific crimes against the Almighty include: empty gestures of offerings (1:11), a disregard for justice toward the people (1:12), and the meaningless gestures of prayer (1:13-15). Bad moral conduct had been hidden behind the disingenuous overtures of prayer and religious ritual. In short, the people said one thing, but lived a life of hypocrites.

The Creator advises the people of Israel to "learn to do good, seek justice, rescue the oppressed, defend the orphan, plead for the widow" (Isaiah 1:17). Or the Almighty will "pour out my wrath on my enemies" who have ignored justice and are "now murders," who are princes that have become "rebels and companions of thieves," for "everyone who loves a bribe and runs after gifts," who "do not defend the orphan," and for ignoring "the widow's cause" that "does not come before them" (1:21-24).

Hubris by the religious and political elite added to God's displeasure with Israel. The Governor of the Universe urges the House of Jacob to "walk in the light of the Lord" (Isaiah 2:5)! The leadership has "forsaken the ways of your people" (2:6). "Their land is filled with idols; they bow down to the work of their hands, to what their own fingers have made." The Creator declares that the "haughtiness of people shall be humbled" (2:17). This is the behavior likened to Sodom and Gomorrah.

Addressing Orthodoxy's concerns about homosexuality cannot be done with a Western styled approach to theology. Although there are similarities and even some overlap, they are distinct. Among Orthodox Church scholars theology goes beyond a scientific methodology. There is an expectation that there is a living communion with the Giver of Life.

The equation must include a collective apostolic tradition involving the handing down of sources from learned Desert Fathers who are witnesses to the living tradition of Jesus. Hence, any proper approach must start from the beginning. It must be crafted with a sensitivity that respects a theological lineage from the past to the present that reflects the timeless, living word of God.

It is critical to remember that today's Orthodox leaders are concerned that something is being added to the Church's long established witness from popular or new age culture. In doing so, the Resurrection, the central witness to Christianity, is disgraced in some minds.

Irenaeus tells a story of a craftsman who uses beautiful, valuable jewels to make an image of a monarch. Another person takes this work of art and breaks it apart. He then orders the stones into the likeness of a small animal. According to Fr. George Florovsky

(1893-1979), "This is precisely what the heretics do with the Scripture."[xlvi] He believed that the truth is "dismembered."

It is the Orthodox Church, the community of leaders and their flocks, that is the keeper of the apostolic traditions and the interpreters of scripture. Hence, efforts to have its leaders examine or re-examine will not be easy. It is important to note, however, that bishops may publicly express "personal theological opinions," as I have done here, which are not binding on greater Orthodoxy.[xlvii] Throughout history priests, bishops, and patriarchs have modified their understanding of scripture as the Holy Spirit revealed greater Truth to them. Truth did not change. They did.

It's important that the Church leadership as a whole understand that tradition and long accepted doctrinal definitions would not be changed to accommodate gay and lesbian spirituality and civil rights. It would not be a pursuit of relativism. Nor will there be any radical shift in Orthodox ecclesiology regarding the nature and function of the Church. The Church is sacred, but there must be a degree of humility in recognizing that its leaders are human. Orthodox clergy and prelates, like Roman Catholic and Protestant counterparts, have been wrong in the past.

The Church represents the whole truth. It is the true life and the life of truth. Individual bishops cannot infallibly proclaim this truth. According to Sergius Bulgakov (1871-1944), a hierarchy "placed above the people, that is, outside them, separated form them, is no more capable of proclaiming the truth of the Church."[xlviii]

Think about the documented affiliation between the notorious KGB and Patriarch Alexy II of the Russian Orthodox Moscow Patriarchate. Leaders in the collective body of the church that appears to be with, among, and part of the people can be flawed and thus Church pronouncements must be respectfully questioned because Christ challenges us to do so. If His disciples did not question and challenge contemporary institutional thinking throughout history then how could there be justice?

Each Orthodox priest and bishop must be approached and educated as to why gay and lesbian rights are in keeping with Orthodox apostolic tradition. Can a handful of priests or bishops change the Orthodox world view? No. Yet an increasing number pushing the envelope can do so over time. One need only look to the canonical Finnish Orthodox Church of the Ecumenical Patriarchate.

The ideas and philosophy of Aleksandr Bukharev (1824-1871), considered by some as Orthodoxy's first modern theologian and who had been censored by the Orthodox Church for a time, should be revisited. He and others did not deal with issues like an open debate about homosexuality, but his method of thinking, processing, and reflecting on theological issues merit exploration and possibly use in today's world. Bukharev, had a fresh, unconventional approach to the challenges that Orthodoxy and the faithful faced in a rapidly changing world.

Bukharev sought a religious renewal that nurtured an awakening to a higher spiritual level. In his day, Orthodoxy seemed stuck at a crossroads where it preserved its traditions, as if housed in a museum, rather than respect and celebrate oneness with God in a way that went beyond ceremony and energetic spiritual thinking.[xlix]

Ukrainian theologian and philosopher Hryhorij Savyc Skovoroda (1722-94) found a means to balance Orthodox Christianity with the Age of the Enlightenment. Unlike many philosophers during the Age of Enlightenment who belittled and criticized Christians and Christianity, he remained a disciple of Jesus. He made a distinction between belief in Christ and the secular, ceremonial trappings of organized religion that contributed to priestcraft, superstition, and ostentatious fancy dress that distanced people from God.

He viewed scripture as symbolic and allegorical. Skovoroda approached scripture with logic, common sense, and a belief that it was consistent with the natural world. Biblical literalism, he believed, rebelled "against the realm of her [nature's] laws." Such a rebellion was "impertinence which loves obstruction, impossibility and uselessness and is the adversary of utility." He deemed superstition that arose from this rebellion as worse than atheism because there is nothing "more bitter and brutal than superstition and nothing is more impudent that a superstitious rage...this rage murderously persecutes its own brothers and with this thinks that it is giving service to God."[l]

In 1760, he declined a request by the Bishop of Belgorod to be tonsured a monk calling it a "monkish masquerade." Skovoroda, a wanderer for much of his life, said he had no desire to add to the ranks of the Pharisees to "eat richly, drink sweetly, dress softly and monk about!"[li]

Skovoroda described his theological approach to scripture with a parable. He tells of a hermit who lived in "deepest isolation." Every morning the pious man entered his garden and attempted to catch a "fair and gentle bird." Try as he may the hermit could not capture the bird.

A guest asked the hermit how he manages not to die of boredom in such isolation. The pious man responded that he has "the bird and the beginning. I hunt the bird, but never catch him. I have a thousand and one ornate silken knots. I seek their beginning, but cannot find it."[lii]

Here Skovoroda underscores God's revelation to humankind, but at the same time the incomprehensible mystery that is the Maker of All Good. It is in keeping with apophatic theology, the inability to fully understand the mystery of the Supreme Ruler. He is intellectually awed by the mysteries of Christ. And it is in the mysteries that he hungers for greater revelations of truth, the sum of which he can never obtain. It is his personal sojourn toward the Creator.

The Holy One is unsearchable and unfathomable (Job 11:7-8; Acts 17:23; Romans 11:33-36). Is it possible that another chapter in the revelation of truth is occurring regarding God's LGBTS children? If it is not occurring should it not at least be thoroughly explored so that the issue can be put to rest?

Perhaps the All-Knowing Creator calls us to an apophatic theology combined with hesychasm to reflect, be still, and ask the difficult questions regarding what seems to be a growing affront to faith and personal dignity that will not subside. It should never be forgotten that Orthodox hermeneutics calls us to use spiritual discernment along with humility, recognizing that a long-held biblical interpretation could be incorrect.

Sensitivity is warranted when calling LGBTS children "evil" or their behavior "evil." Words wound and cause enormous spiritual and emotional damage. It has made some doubt the value of their personhood and the Lord's unconditional love.

"Failure to recognize one's own absolute significance," writes Solovyov, "is equivalent to a denial of human worth…If one is so faint-hearted that he is powerless even to believe in himself, how can he believe in anything else?"[liii] No one should be made to feel this way.

Such descriptions also call into question the historic, dramatic, and ongoing positive impact and influence that gays and lesbians have on art, ballet, music, theater, literature, and especially religion.

Hellenistic society widely accepted homosexuality. Known gay men like Plato had a significant, profound impact on the thinking of the Desert Fathers. Plato's influence continues to influence Christianity to this day. Active homosexuals like Michelangelo and Leonardo Da Vinci defined religious art. What of Tchaikovsky? He was a gay man, unbeknownst to Russian or Ukrainian society today, who crafted music for the Divine Liturgy. The list goes on.[liv]

Clearly, society did not suffer due to gays and lesbians, but benefitted. This is one of many reasons why the LGBTS Christian witness is already part of the Church. Furthermore, if Orthodoxy can shift its attitudes toward slavery, serfdom, and anti-Semitism, among other things, then it can do the same regarding homosexuality.

ANTI-SEMITISM

John Chrysostom, the "Doctor of the Church," laid some foundations for anti-Semitism that continues to this day in a number of branches of Orthodoxy. Of particular note are eight homilies that ravaged Jews in what one historian noted was "with a bitterness and lack of restraint unusual even in that place and century." Although Christianity was firmly rooted and Jews already started to be legally segregated away from the rest of the community, Chrysostom's anti-Semitism is notable.

This Church Father, also known as "golden-mouthed" for his eloquent preaching, referred to the Jewish people as "sensual, slippery, voluptuous, avaricious, possessed by demons, drunkards, harlots, and breakers of the Law."[lv] His treatment of Jews led to the incorporation of anti-Semitic passages in the Divine Liturgy.

Fortunately, most Orthodox Churches have done the unthinkable. They altered the Divine Liturgy by removing offensive, anti-Semitic passages inspired by the traditions of a Church Father. Did God change? Did Orthodoxy succumb to relativism, secularism, or become untrue to sacred traditions? No. Instead, it moved closer to the fullness of God.

Today, however, some Orthodox Churches still use theology to justify anti-Semitism. In addition, despite the changes cited above, there are parts of the world where anti-Semitism is still found in the Divine Liturgy in use. This includes referring to Jews as "Christ-killers" and calling for revenge.[lvi]

In 2004, three anti-Semitic books were published by the Belorussian Orthodox Church Moscow Patriarchate.[lvii] In January 2005, the U.S. State Department issued a report citing the Greek Orthodox Church in Greece for its complacency toward anti-Semitism. One example cited involved the burning of an effigy of Judas at Easter among some parishes.[lviii]

"We are an Orthodox country," said the priest inciting a mob to tear down a menorah placed in a public square in December 2009.

"Stephan the Great [of Moldova] defended our country from all kinds of kikes."[lix] The official statement by the Moldova Orthodox Church, which called the incident "unfortunate," gave the following rationale: "We think it inappropriate to put a symbol of the Jewish cult in a public place connected to the history and faith of our people, especially because Chanukah is classified by the cult books of Judaism as a 'holiday of blessing' that symbolizes the victory of Jews over non-Jews."[lx] Most of the Orthodox world including churches in the West said nothing.

Not surprisingly, Chrysostom held equal contempt for men who had sex with men. No other Church Father wrote or spoke more about it than him, which laid the foundations for the prejudice that continues throughout the Christian world. According to Chrysostom, homosexuals were "even worse than murderers…" They were "monstrous," "Satanical," "detestable," "execrable," and "pitiable."[lxi]

Orthodoxy now, like Orthodoxy yesterday regarding anti-Semitism, links the synodical canons and Patristic pronouncements on homosexuality back to Chrysostom. Clearly, as in the case of anti-Semitism, synodical canons and Patristic pronouncements were revised in parts of the Orthodox world because the Holy Spirit has revealed a greater truth.

Do not confuse the tradition of men with the holiness of scripture and the tradition of Christ's love (Mark 7:8). The tradition of God never changes. The tradition of men does and must. "Beware lest anyone cheat you…according to the tradition of men…and not according to Christ" (Colossians 2:8).

In 2009, a blogger with a degree from a Ukrainian college pursuing graduate work in the United States commented on the controversy surrounding whether Sir Elton and his spouse should be allowed to adopt a child from Ukraine. The blogger noted that not only are a majority of Ukrainians homophobic, but they'd rather "accept you" as Jewish then gay.[lxii]

SERFDOM AND SLAVERY

The Eastern Orthodox Church at one time supported serfdom. Human beings became attached to the land and faced a myriad of physical and emotional abuse. St. Tikhon of Zadonsk, one of the great saints of Orthodoxy, wrote that serfs should "submit to authorities." He called masters the servants of God who should be obeyed. Serfs "must submit to their masters, doing the will of God from their soul."[lxiii]

The Church even supported slavery. Roma or Gypsies were forced to work in Romanian Orthodox monasteries. They were owned and sold at will by the Church.[lxiv] Slavery existed in the Ukrainian provinces of Bukovina and parts of Galicia. In 1783, efforts by the Roman Emperor to abolish the practice met with fierce opposition, especially from Romanian Orthodox monasteries.[lxv] In Russia widespread slavery existed before it became serfdom.[lxvi]

Orthodox leaders of the day justified ownership of human beings citing Ephesians 6:5; 1 Timothy 6:1, Titus 2:9-10 and Leviticus 25:44-46. It bears repeating that the Book of Leviticus is still cited today to condemn gays and lesbians. In the eyes of the Church, faith saved the individual from sin, not physical or secular freedom.

A Christian, according to Fr. Alexander Men (1935-1990), "is not afraid to look critically at the Church's past…knows that liturgical rules and canon law have changed over the centuries and cannot remain absolutely unaltered in the future. This also applies to the theological interpretation of the truths of the faith. Such interpretation has had a long history, and has passed through phases when more of the truth was revealed and when interpretation deepened."[lxvii]

This theological approach leads to a more spiritually, religiously, and intellectually honest discussion of any issue. He didn't see threats to the Church. Fr. Men, mysteriously murdered on his way to celebrate the Divine Liturgy at his church outside Moscow, viewed perceived threats or challenges as opportunities to show the strength of the Church and one's faith in it. He believed atheism was a chance to show the wonders, mysteries, and everlasting beauty that is Christianity.

Although Fr. John Meyendorff (1926-1992) would not necessarily agree with the growing expressions of homosexual acceptance, his observations about Orthodox theological study in America also merit being considered here. He noted that American religiosity reflected "relatively small religious groups" who "claim to possess the truth, affirm that salvation has reached their members (and not other groups), and rejoice in their exclusivity and uniqueness." Meyendorff said that even among the Orthodox there are those who would be comfortable in adopting such an approach.[lxviii]

For these Orthodox, according to Meyendorff, it would "free them from the obligation to listen to others and from the effort needed to look at themselves as others look at them. It would make it unnecessary to draw the line between holy tradition and the human traditions inherited form history, and it would reduce theology to straight affirmations, repeating that which was supposedly 'always said.'"

He adds that such an approach "exclude[s] real theology" and actually renounces "the true traditions of the Fathers." More important this means of doing theology would "align the Orthodox psychologically with the most extreme forms of Protestant fundamentalism."[lxix]

Approaching homosexuality should not be done through anyone's personal or institutional "vision." Let there not be created a forced-truth producing a plastic, artificial spirituality. All in this debate must seek to be on the side of the One Truth. This is in keeping with the approach of one of Orthodoxy's great theologians, Fr. Alexander Men.[lxx]

No matter where this journey leads the core Christian message of – love God and love one another – will not change. Walk with Divine Wisdom (the Holy Spirit) and know that all will be well. She is the breath of the Maker of All Good and the pure oxygen of faith.

SCIENCE

Although countless scientific studies by credible and well-respected sources have shown that homosexuality is a normal part of God's universal order and that same-sex partners make good parents, Orthodoxy rejects these findings believing that there has been an overemphasis on science, thus undermining tradition, Patristic teachings, and the experience of revelation.

Bulgakov wrote that science "is actually born of [Christianity]." Hence, if used responsibly and with humility recognizing that God remains the Creator, then knowledge and improving the quality of life is part of the universal plan.[lxxi] Science has the potential to neutralize fear and nurture greater love among God's children.

Yet putting aside such views and the positions and scientific findings of groups like the American Psychiatric Association[lxxii] the American Psychological Association[lxxiii], Mental Health America (formerly the National Mental Health Association)[lxxiv], National Association of Social Workers, and the support for gay adoptions by the American Academy of Pediatrics[lxxv] among many others, Orthodoxy will not be in conflict with scientific investigation since the results highlighted above can be achieved through its theological perspective.

The 1848 Encyclical of the Eastern Patriarchs, in response to an Epistle of Pope Pius IX, speaks of the whole Church.[lxxvi] This wholeness includes *all of the people no matter their sexual identity*. Hence, excluding the LGBTS faithful does not complete the Church. Instead, it puts obstacles in the way delaying their spiritual journey toward *theosis* or deification.[lxxvii]

Saying that LGBTS Christians are without such a genuine Christian faith experience is incorrect. In order to see this journey, Church leaders must be engaged with the community. Remember Jesus interacted and had genuine fellowship with the least regarded classes of his time. Orthodoxy provides spiritual therapy that cures sin. Gay civil and human rights are expanding, not diminishing throughout the world both in society and among Christian denominations.

Nikolai Berdyaev (1874-1948) reminds Church leaders that a "single Orthodox individual can be more correct than the predominant majority of bishops."[lxxviii]

ETHICS

There is also a role for Orthodox ethics in this debate. Orthodoxy approaches ethics from a soteriolgical perspective (salvation) beginning with the Holy Trinity. The supreme bond of this family is love.

Hence, there should be a closer examination of the absence of dialogue. Why does it exist? In addition, the love two people of the same sex share merits exploration. As noted earlier there is a need to shift focus away from the physical act.

Orthodox ethics is also grounded in Jesus as a person. Can a gay or lesbian person reach communion with God through Christ and still be in a loving same-sex relationship? How is it possible for the most vocal opponents of LGBTS rights to answer that question without getting to know these Christians? The Orthodox Church believes that there is an ongoing journey to be closer to God. How is this possible when some children of the Maker of All Good are ostracized in secular and religious society?

Ethics remains an unaddressed issue in this discussion.

CONCLUSION

The Orthodox Church can, without compromising the organic whole of tradition or Patristic teachings, and without subordinating faith to science, utilize an ontological (human intelligence and intuition emanating from God) pneumatology (of the Holy Spirit) in establishing fellowship with the LGBTS community.

"Orthodoxy," according to Berdyaev "is a greater revelation of the Holy Spirit." He said that "within the depth of Orthodoxy there is always a great expectation of a new religious manifestation in the world, an outpouring of the Holy Spirit…Divine Energy is poured out upon the natural world, acts upon it and enlightens it. This is the Orthodox understanding of the Holy Spirit."[lxxix]

At one time Orthodoxy supported slavery and serfdom. The sun revolved around the earth and God made the universe in six days instead of the millions we now know. It believed that some women could fly on brooms and turn themselves into demonic creatures. These views are no longer held today.

Did Orthodoxy change? No. Did it have a scholastic historical evolution? No. Were there intellectualisms imposed on the Church? No. Were there innovations of human thought? No. Orthodoxy turned more "towards the Kingdom of God" which came about from "the mystical transfiguration of the world."[lxxx] The Holy Spirit made this happen.

The reader is urged to reread Proverbs 8 and 9 and compare the actions of God's Breath to those of the Holy Spirit in the New Testament. The gradual revelation of the Divine Truth is shared with humanity when it shows a collective spiritual maturity (Hebrews 1:1-2). God never changes, but our understanding of the Holy One does.

The Holy Spirit is humanity's guide, mentor, and teacher. (Proverbs 8:22-31), and awakens a greater understanding within individuals and humanity when we listen to the subtle ways of the Spirit (Proverbs 9). Throughout history the Holy Spirit has enabled individuals and all humanity to experience the vision of God. The Holy Spirit is the comforter to those in need.

Christianity tells us that the spiritual journey of an individual or an institution toward the truth can be stormy, confusing, discomforting, and unpredictable. The disciples of Jesus were all confronted with these challenges as they walked with Our Lord as he revealed a purer, greater truth. Let us have courage to acknowledge that the LGBTS Orthodox Christian witness is already part of the Church. It needs to be embraced.

Pierre Teilhard de Chardin, Roman Catholic priest, theologian and paleontologist, reflected that after humankind masters the winds, waves, and gravity, it might "harness the energies of love. And then, for the second time in the history of the world, we will have discovered fire."[lxxxi]

The unconditional love Jesus brought over two thousand years ago is the First Fire. The Second Coming of Fire would be nearer, if only God's universal family would choose love over hate, faith over fear, compassion over indifference, and knowledge over ignorance. This would be "correct or true belief." It would be Orthodoxy at its best.

BISHOP PAUL PETER JESEP, by appointment of His Beatitude Metropolitan Myfodii of Kyiv and All Ukraine, is Director of Public Affairs for the Ukrainian Autocephalous Orthodox Church (UAOC) Kyiv-Patriarchate in the United States. The views and opinions expressed here are solely his own and do not in any way reflect the teachings of the UAOC or any other Orthodox Church.

The only representative of the Orthodox community to participate in the Interfaith Processional of The Right Rev. V. Gene Robinson of the New Hampshire Episcopal Diocese was Bishop Jesep.

Bishop Jesep graduated magna cum laude with a B.A. in political science from Union College in New York. He earned a J.D. from Western New England College School of Law in Massachusetts; a Master's from the Graduate School of Political Management now based at George Washington University; and earned a Master's degree from Bangor Theological Seminary in Maine. In addition to practicing law in New York State, he is author of *Crucifying Jesus and Secularizing America – the Republic of Faith without Wisdom*. He may be reached at VladykaPaulPeter@aol.com.

NOTES

[i] *Against the Heresies* -- http://www.newadvent.org/fathers/0103.htm.
[ii] Used as a reference throughout this essay is George W. Grube, *The Complete Book of Orthodoxy* (Salisbury, MA: Regina Orthodox Press, 2001).
[iii] See in general Vladimir Solovyov, *Lectures on Divine Humanity* (Hudson, NY: Lindisfarne Press, 1995).
[iv] The Finnish Orthodox Church has been widely perceived as being more open to revisiting whether long-held views on homosexuality that could be based on misinterpretations of scripture. Clergy have encouraged parishioners to have an open discussion about the issue. The Russian Orthodox Church Moscow-Patriarchate with its uncompromising condemnation of homosexuality has threatened to establish a diocese in Finland. See "The Question About Homosexuals is Complicating Relationships Between the Orthodox in Russia and Finland," http://sateenkaariseura.wordpress.com/articles-from-other-sites/the-question-about-homosexuals-2032007, 20 March 2007.
The Finnish Orthodox Church also participated in the European Forum of LGBT Christian Groups Conference Courage in May 2009. See "Finnish Orthodox Church and Homosexuality," Kimisis.net, 22 May 2009.
[v] "Russian Chapel Razed After Gay 'Marriage,'" *Washington Times*, 9 October 2003. See also "Nizhny Novgorod Church in Which Homosexuals Married Demolished," Portal-Credo.ru, 7 October 2003.
[vi] Ibid., "Nizhny Novgorod Church in Which Homosexuals Married Demolished."
[vii] The relationship His Holiness has had with the Communists "led to accusations that he was too closely identified with implementing the government's anti-religious policies. Documents show he fulfilled KGB commands in quelling protests among monks at the Pskov Monastery of the Caves." A British newspaper reported that he had been described as "in the category of bishops most loyal to the Soviet state. His reporting and implementation of the state's wishes brought him a secret KGB award in February 1988." See Felix Corley, "Patriarch Alexy II: Priest who Stayed Close to the Kremlin while Guiding the Russian Orthodox Church into the Post-Soviet Era," Independent.co.uk, 6 December 2008. See also "Russian Patriarch 'was KGB Spy'," Guardian.co.uk, 12 February 1997 and Megan K. Stack, "Russian Orthodox Patriarch Alexei II, 79, Dies in Moscow, LATimes.com, 6 December 2008.

Perhaps the most damning evidence came from Konstantin Preobrazhensky, a former Lt. Colonel in the KGB, who charged that "the leadership of the Moscow Patriarchate all were members of the Communist Party, which has been skillfully concealed." According to him dictator Joseph Stalin "created the Moscow Patriarchate with the hands of the KGB. This department became her mother. The genetic ties with the KGB in the Moscow Patriarchate are just as strong as the times between [the] Russian Orthodox Church Outside Russia (ROCOR) and the White anti-Communist Movement . . . Bishops were part of the nomenclature of the CK KPSS (Central Committee of the Communist Party of the Soviet Union), therefore each individual had to be approved by the Ideological Department." The KGB determined who could be approved for elevation from priest to bishop.

This determination was made, in part, based on the damaging personal information that the KGB kept in their files. "The Moscow Patriarchate," says Preobrazhensky, "is amazing merciful toward murderers fulfilling presidential orders. In 2004, Aleksey II awarded Dmitry Pavlichenko, a Colonel of the Belorussian Special Services, with the Medal of the Equal-to-the-Apostles Prince Vladimir. He was the infamous organizer of the 'squadrons of death' which liquidated political enemies of President Lukashenko [of Byelorussia]. This excerpt was taken from the website of The Centre for Counterintelligence and Security Studies (CI Centre). It is from Preobrazhensky's book, *Russian Americans: A New KGB Asset.*

Church-Communist collaboration began in 1927. Metropolitan Sergy (Stragorodsky) submitted the Church to the KGB. The Church became a tool to advance many Communist principles. The selection of bishops had to be approved by the KGB who kept dossiers on priests with any embarrassing information. All bishops were expected to act on behalf of the KGB when asked. Named after the Metropolitan himself the submission became know as *Sergiyanstvo*. See in general: John Garrard and Carol Garrard, *Russian Orthodoxy Resurgent: Faith and Power in the New Russia* (Princeton: Princeton University Press, 2008).

[viii] "Patriarch Alexy of Russia Assails Gays in Speech at Council of Europe," *New York Times*, 2 October 2007.

[ix] Ibid.

[x] See in general: Louis Crompton, Homosexuality & Civilization (Cambridge: The Belknap Press of Harvard University Press, 2003).

[xi] Independent of Alexy II's collaboration with the Soviet secret police (KGB) and his continued work with President Vladimir Putin, there have been sex and financial scandals plaguing the Church leadership. See in general: "Metropolitan Herman Responds to Archbishop[Dmitri," Press Release posted by the Orthodox Church of America, 30 March 2007, OCA.org; "Disgraced Greek Bishop Faces Trial on Money Laundering Charges," *Christianity Today*, 14 April 2005; and Helen Smith, "Sex and Fraud Woe for Greek Church," 19 February 2005, Guardian.com.

[xii] Victor Yasmann, "Russia: The Orthodox Church and the Kremlin's New Mission," Radio Free Euope, (RFERL.org) April 10, 2006.

[xiii] Fyodor Dostoevsky, *The Brothers Karamazov* (New York: Bantam Books, 1981), at 297-319.

[xiv] Aydar Buribayev and Amie Ferris-Rotman, "Moscow Bans 'Satanic' Gay Parade on Eurovision Day," Reuters, 8 May 2009.

[xv] "Russian Police Arrest Gay Demonstrators Ahead of Songfest," MonstersandCritics.com, 16 May 2009.

[xvi] "Russia Authorities Pressuring Civil Groups, Condoning Rights Abuses, Hate Crimes: Amnesty," KyivPost.com, 23 May 2007.

[xvii] Ina R. Friedman, *The Other victims – First-Person Stories of Non- Jews Persecuted by the Nazis*, Boston: Houghton Mifflin Company, 1990, at 25.

[xviii] Joshua Cinelli, "Church in Ukraine Calls Elton John a 'Sinner' in Adoption Inquiry," *New York Daily News*, 16 September 2009.

[xix] Ukraine has "the fastest-rising HIV infection rate in Europe." See "Sir Elton John's Adoption Hopes Dashed by Ukraine," Telegraph.co.uk, 14 September

2009. According to a social worker at the All-Ukrainian Network of People Living with HIV/AIDS, as quoted by the BBC, "there are some 8,000 HIV-affected children in Ukraine. Out of them, 2,000 are HIV positive and some 500 [out of HIV positive] are orphans." See "Nation Snubs Elton John's Attempt to Adopt Orphan," There are over 31,000 children in Ukrainian orphanages waiting for adoption. KyivPost.com, 17 September 2009.

xx   Ibid., "Nation Snubs Elton John's Attempt to Adopt Orphan."
xxi   Will Stewart, "Elton John 'is a sinner': Church Attacks Singer Over His Plan to Adopt Ukrainian Baby Boy," DailyMail.co.uk, 16 September 2009.
xxii   "Ukrainians Demand Imprisonment for Gay Propaganda," ChristianTelegraph.com, 17 August 2009.
xxiii   "Ukrainian Scholars Criticize Homosexuality on Biblical Grounds," RISU.org., 26 December 2005.
xxiv   Ibid. Documented discrimination faced by gays and lesbians in Ukraine is found in *Ukrainian Homosexuals and Society*, issued by Nash Mir (Our World) of the Gay and Lesbian Center in Kyiv, Gay.org.ua.
xxv   There is an ironic twist to the story. Yuri Pavlenko, Youth and Sports Minister of Ukraine, who deemed Sir Elton and Mr. Furnish unacceptable parents said that they have "the right and opportunity to invite the family of this boy to visit him, take them under his guardianship and help him grow into a good person." See "Celebrity Baby Scoop: Elton John is Given some Hope," KyivPost.com, 19 September 2009. The "sinners" still have the moral standing to help raise the child to be "a good person."
xxvi   "Homosexuality and the Church: An Address to the Coptic Orthodox Priests in England," OrthodxyToday.org, 19 June 2008.
xxvii   The Pope's approach is disturbing for at least two reasons. First, citing the Hebrew Scripture's use of death for homosexual acts suggests that the punishment should be brought back.. Otherwise, why even raise it? Or is he suggesting that gays and lesbians should be grateful that it is no longer used? He seems to be a half-hearted literalist or perhaps unsure as to what a divinely inspired text is and the timelessly message it offers in a modern world. The fact that he draws attention to a punishment that civilized society now deems reprehensible, even in Israel today, suggests that the Hebrew Scriptures have significant limitations thus potentially undermining their credibility on other matters of faith. In referencing this punishment in Leviticus he draws attention to other scriptural passages long since ignored and for good reason: an "unclean" woman due to menstruation or child birth is forbidden to enter a sanctuary or touch "any hallowed thing" (Leviticus 12:1-4); transfer sins of the children of Israel to a goat set loose in the desert, hence the term "scapegoat" (Leviticus 16:20-21); heterosexual adulterers are to be put to death (Leviticus 20:10-11); the person who takes the Lord's name in vain shall be put to death (Leviticus 24:16); and as for slaves "you may buy some of the children of sojourners dwelling among you, and some of their families with you, which they beget in your land; and they shall become your possession. You may also distribute them as an inheritance for your children after you" (Leviticus 25:45-46). In citing the death penalty for homosexuals His Holiness has forgotten the lessons of the Holocaust. Hitler planned to exterminate all gays and

lesbians. Many died in the camps, were sterilized, used for experiments, or faced brutality in prisons. See in general Ina R. Friedman, *The Other victims – First-Person Stories of Non-Jews Persecuted by the Nazis*, Boston: Houghton Mifflin Company, 1990, Heinz Heger, *The Men with the Pink Triangle – the True, Life-and-Death Story of Homosexuals in the Nazi Death Camps* (Boston: Alyson Publications, 1994), Richard Plant, *The Nazi War Against Homosexuals – Pink Triangle* (New York: Henry Holt and Company, 1988). "Paragraph 175," A Rob Epstein & Jeffrey Friedman Film narrated by Rupert Everett, NewYorkerFilms.com. Any time someone brings up the Hebrew scriptural punishment of death should be publicly reminded that Hitler sought the same solution.

[xxviii] Ibid.

[xxix] "Gay Parade in Serbia Canceled," Serbianna.com, 19 September 2009.

[xxx] Marius Zaharia, "Romania Debates Religion's Role in Schools," Times of Malta.com, 18 August 2008.

[xxxi] "Clashes Mark Romanian Gay Parade," New.BBC.co.uk, 6 April 2006.

[xxxii] Peter Kostadinov, "More Religious Leaders Want the Rainbow Friendship March Banned," SofiaEcho.com, 27 June 2009.

[xxxiii] "Q.A. What is the viewpoint of the Armenian Apostolic Church on Homosexuality?" MyPriest.Araratian-tem.am/showquest.php?id=18.

[xxxiv] "Belarusian Gays, Lesbians Want to Take Part in Path of Chornobyl Procession," KyivPost.com, 23 April 2009.

[xxxv] "Texts of the Agreed Statements of the Joint Commission," CopticChurch.org/node/373.

[xxxvi] "The Seventh Meeting of the Heads of the Oriental Orthodox Churches in the Middle East," St. Mark Centre, Nasr City, Cairo, Egypt, 20-21 October 2004, sor.cua.edu.

[xxxvii] See Fr. Mikhail E. Mikhail, *Introduction and Conclusion of the Coptic Orthodox Church's View on Homosexuality*, www.stmarkcocleveland.org and "The Coptic Orthodox Church and Homosexuality," ReligiousTolerance.org.

[xxxviii] Ukrainian Orthodox Church of Canada, UOCC.ca/en-ca/faith/beliefs/.

[xxxix] "SCOBA Statement on Moral Crisis in Our Nation," goarch.org/news/goa.news971, 27 August 2003.

[xl] Ibid.

[xli] "On Same-Sex Unions Epistle of the ROCOR W. Diocese," OrthodoxInfo.com, 2004.

[xlii] Yhteys (Unity), which advocates on behalf of sexual minority rights, organized the event. Keynote speakers and their topics were: Prof. Kerstin Soderblom, Goether University Frankfurt, *The European Churches and their Sexual Minorities*; The Rt. Rev. Wille Riekkinen, *How to Define a Theological Stand on Homosexuality*; The Rev. Heikki Huttunen, General Secretary of the Ecumenical Counsel of Finland, *Human Sexuality in the Orthodox Theology*; and Prof Vesa Hirvonen, *Does Homosexuality Challenge the Doctrine of the Church?*

[xliii] Prof. Hirvonen graciously provided a copy of his lecturer for reference here.

[xliv] Interview with Archbishop Leo, "Gay Sexuality," 2008. *Aamun Koitto*, Aamunkoitto.fi.

[xlv] See in General John Meyendorff, "Doing Theology in an Eastern Orthodox Perspective," *Eastern Orthodox Theology – A Contemporary Reader*, Edited by Daniel B. Clendenin. Grand Rapids: Baker Books, 2002. See also Daniel L. Migliore, *Faith Seeking Understanding*. Grand Rapids: William B. Eerdmans Publishing Company, 2004.

[xlvi] Fr. George Florovsky, "The Function of Tradition in the Ancient Church," essay in *Eastern Orthodox Theology*, ed. By Daniel B. Clendenin (Grand Rapids: Baker Academic, 2003), at 101.

[xlvii] Sergius Bulgakov, *The Orthodox Church* (Crestwood, New York: St. Vladimir's Seminary Press, 1988), at 56.

[xlviii] Ibid., at 59.

[xlix] Paul Valliere, *Modern Russian Theology – Bukharev, Soloviev, Bulgakov – Orthodox Theology in a New Key*, Grand Rapids: William B. Eerdmans Publishing Company, 2000, at 19-106.

[l] Stephen P. Scherer, "Enlightenment Elements in the Thought of Hryhorij Skovoroda," *Michigan Academician*, 22 March 2008 (printed from AccessMyLibrary.com).

[li] Ibid.

[lii] Richard H. Marshall, Jr. and Thomas E. Bird, eds. *Hryhorij Savyc Skovoroda* (Edmonton: Canadian Institute of Ukrainian Studies Press, 1994), at 54-55.

[liii] Vladimir Solovyov, *The Meaning of Love* (Hudson: Lindisfarne Press, 1985), at 43.

[liv] See in general Robert Aldrich, *Who's Who in Gay and Lesbian History from Antiquity to World War II* (London: Routledge, 2001); Robert Aldrich, *Gay Life and Culture: A World History* (London: Universe, 2006); John Boswell, *Christianity, Social Tolerance, and Homosexuality* (Chicago: University of Chicago Press, 1981); B.R. Burg, ed., *Gay Warriors – A Documentary History from the Ancient World to the Present* (New York: New York University Press, 2002); Louis Crompton, Homosexuality & Civilization (Cambridge: Belknap Press, 2003); and Byrne Fone, *Homophobia – A History* (New York: Metropolitan Book, 2000).

[lv] Louis Crompton, *Homosexuality & Civilization* (Cambridge: Belknap Press of Harvard University, 2003), p. 139. See also http://www.fordham.edu/halsall/source/chrysostom-jews6.html.

[lvi] "ADL Urges Orthodox Christian Churches to Excise Anti-Semitism from the Liturgy,"Anti-Defamation League (ADL.org) press release, 6 June 2007. See also "To Recognize Christ in His People – The Final Declaration by the Christian Round Table of Eastern Orthodox Priests and Cultural Representatives form Greece, Georgia, Italy, Russia, and Ukraine Visiting Jerusalem," Jewish-Christian Relations (JCRelations.net), April; 20-24, 2007. See in general: Robert Louis Wilken, *John Chrysostom and the Jews: Rhetoric and Reality in the Late Fourth Century* (Berkeley: University of California Press, 1983) and Paul W. Harkins, translator, *John Chrysostom, Discourses Against Judaizing Christians* (Washington: Catholic University of America Press, 1979). See also http://www.fordham.edu/halsall/source/chrysostom-jews6.html.

[lvii] Yuras Karmanau, "Jewish Leader Says Belarus Leadership Turns Blind Eye to Anti-Semitism," AP Worldstream (AccessMyLibrary.com), 17 March 2005.

lviii "Archbishop Christodoulos Rejects U.S. State Department Report on Anti-Semitism in Greece," Europe Intelligence Wire (AccessMyLibrary.com), 9 January 2005.
lix "Despicable Anti-Semitic Attack in Moldova Merits Strong Response by Government and Church," Anti-Defamation League (ADL) press release, December 14, 2009.
lx "Moldovan Orthodox Church: Jews to Blame for Menorah Incident," YNETNews.com, December 23, 2009.
lxi Louis Crompton, *Homosexuality & Civilization* (Cambridge: Belknap Press of Harvard University Press, 2003), at 141.
lxii Leo Krasnozhon, "Ukraine Seriously Needs Harvey Milk," 24 September 2009, UkraineWatch.blogspot.com.
lxiii St. Tikhon of Zadonsk, Journey to Heaven (Jordanville, New York: Holy Trinity Monastery, 1994), p. 127.
lxiv Alexandru Alexe, "Romanian Gypsies Celebrate 150 Years Since Emancipation, Demand Apologies for Slavery," AP Worldstream (AccessMyLibrary.org), 20 February 2006.
lxv "Slavery in Romania," Wikipedia.org.
lxvi See in general: Hugh Thomas, *The Slave Trade: The Story of the Atlantic Slave Trade: 1440-1870* (New York: Touchstone, 1999), Adele Lindenmeyr, *Poverty Is Not a Vice: Charity, Society and the State in Imperial Russia* (Princeton: Princeton University Press, 1996). and Richard Hellie, *Slavery in Russia – 1450-1725* (Chicago: University of Chicago, 1982) and *The Economy and Material Culture of Russia 1600-1725* (Chicago: University of Chicago, 1999).
lxvii AlexanderMen.com
lxviii Supra Note 36.
lxix Ibid., 94-95.
lxx Yakov Krotov, "Fr. Aleksandr Men: Christian Priest and Apologist," *East-West Church & Ministry Report* (EastWestReport.org) Vol. 7, No. 3, Summer 1999.
lxxi Bulgakov, *The Orthodox Church* (Crestwood: St. Vladimir's Press, 1988), p. 166
lxxii http://www.healthyminds.org/More-Info-For/GayLesbianBisexuals.aspx.
lxxiii http://www.apa.org/topics/sorientation.html.
lxxiv http://www.mentalhealthamerica.net/index.cfm?objectid=DE58275D-1372-4D20-C8B2877A93FC8373.
lxxv http://aapnews.aappublications.org/cgi/search?journalcode=aapnews&fulltext=homosexual+adoption.
lxxvi See in general *Encyclical of the Eastern Patriarchs, 1848 – A Reply to the Epistle of Pope Pius IX to the Easterns*, OrthodoxInfo.com.
lxxvii See in general John Meyendorff, *St. Gregory Palamas and Orthodox Spirituality* (Crestwood: St. Vladimir's Seminary Press, 1974).
lxxviii Nikolai Berdyaev, "Discord in the Church and Freedom of Conscience," Chebucto.ns.ca/Philosophy/Sui-Generis/Berdyaev/essays/discord.html.
lxxix _____ Berdyaev, "The Truth of Orthodoxy."
lxxx Ibid.

[lxxxi] Pierre Teilhand de Chardin, *Toward the Future* (London: William Collins Sons & Co., 1975), pp. 86-87.

A BRIEF HISTORY
BY FATHER GEORGE BATTELLE

AXIOS - EASTERN & ORTHODOX GAY AND LESBIAN CHRISTIANS

WHY DO I CARE?

I am an Orthodox Christian precisely because I believe the Orthodox Church is the same Church established by Jesus Christ himself, the body that continues to pass on the holy Christian Tradition, wrote and preserved the Holy Scriptures, nurtured the Church Fathers and clarified our faith in, at the very least, seven ecumenical councils. While much of what follows may seem critical of Orthodox Christianity, that is not my intention. I intend this writing to be basically descriptive and factual. I pray each day for knowledge of his will for me and for the strength and willingness to carry that out. I do not consider it my position to judge anyone. I am merely presenting a case, a case for love, compassion, and fairness coupled with sanity that treats adults like adults. We do not have to hide our brains in the closet nor believe that dinosaurs and humans lived at the same time to be Orthodox. Even though the "mind of Christ" was given to the Church at Pentecost, we can still wake up further to it more and more even 2000 years later as we live and work together in the Orthodox community and in our relationships. It is obvious to me that slavery by human masters is not within the mind of Christ. But exclusively literal scriptural interpretations do not help us. We understand through participation in relationships. Whether people are killed in war or killed because they saved seeds, rainwater, or stepped on US land mines, understanding our relationships in the mind of Christ is Orthopraxy. The work of understanding is critical to Orthopraxy.

SEARCHING FOR THE HISTORIC CHURCH

My search for historic Christianity began actually within a very devout Anglican background. My godmother was Darla Hood of the Rascals. Before my voice broke, I sang soprano solos at the

Church of the Advent where the Nat King Cole family attended and I was charmed by Eleanor Roosevelt there. I usually served as acolyte or reader at two services on Sunday. I gravitated to the high churches in Los Angeles and usually attended daily offices when I could. In my youth, I never felt apart from God because of my homosexuality. But I gradually stopped trusting myself and began to believe what I read, at that time, from medical doctors, psychologists, clergy *et al.* that there was no such a thing as a homosexual. There were only heterosexuals, some of whom were sick and needed to hug guys. I was active in the Canterbury Club at UCLA where I had dinner and conversation with my third Archbishop of Canterbury. I was married. I was among 10 men selected to go to England to seminary and then to work in South Africa as priests. I ended up not going out of fear of not being able to keep straight and become a disgrace to my family. Before we had children, I came out to my wife and we decided to stay together. I sought counseling and 'discovered' that my homosexuality was not the problem but my needing to be open and honest about it was. Later, I found that a gay group of Roman Catholics called Dignity held meetings in San Diego. The priest there welcomed me. At that time, we could not gain entrance without our secret membership cards. But we discovered that most of the members were driving down from Los Angeles and the group decided to also hold meetings in Los Angeles. My wife and I offered use of our home. So the first two or three Dignity meetings in Los Angeles were held there and Mass was served on our dining room table. Soon Dignity received permission to use the Newman Center, but was later evicted by the diocese. I felt enough at home there to help Dignity's building fund with a founder's club membership.

Still I didn't feel at home. If it wasn't the gay issue, then it was the intercommunion issue. I had read too much honest Anglican and general Church history from a consular perspective to want to become Roman Catholic. Nevertheless I felt like a weird outsider as an Anglo-Catholic in the Protestant Episcopal Church and, anachronistically enough, I felt a complete lack of support as a gay person. In the United States, the Episcopal Church today is working, even suffering, through an honest orthopraxy on that issue as opposed to the Orthodox Churches who have yet to even begin the work of dialog on this issue.

SAINT SERAPHIM ORTHODOX CHURCH LONG BEACH, CA

During the winter of 1972-1973, I saw an ad for an Orthodox Mission in Long Beach, California, and it was in English. I was drawn to it and within a few minutes of hearing the heavenly choir, I was amazed to actually hear the priest quoting Saint John Chrysostom and Saint Basil. This was like going back in time to the historic church. I was aware that many other churches named their church buildings after saints but here I was actually hearing the words of the saints that seemed like they were living and preaching a faith relevant for today. I was hooked. From then on, I was at every Divine Service and was helping out during the week. In 1973, both of my children and I were chrismated there. Worshiping God at St. Seraphim's was the most spiritually connective and joyful time of my life.

St. Seraphim Orthodox Church began in Long Beach with 3 families and grew to 200 on the mailing list and 70 each Sunday for Divine Liturgy after the patronal festival five years later. This was not an "activist parish" but simply a parish of devout Orthodox Christians according each other mutual love and respect as we worshipped God. The parish priest was very intelligent; however, his written English was less than perfect. He asked me to be the parish newsletter editor, which I was honored to help prepare. That gave me a good opportunity to become acquainted with everyone and sing bass in the choir.

During the entire 6 years I was there, there were only two occasions I ever heard comments made on the topic of homosexuality. Once a very generous and spiritual older lady said to me: "Do you know that D. and T. are gay?...but that is OK." The other time a member of the board inappropriately confided in me that a parishioner was in a hospital for a disease "that gays get." So there was no "scandal" in that parish. And some time before, our priest had assured me that "the Orthodox Church does not excommunicate for that!" I had been temporarily visiting a Greek Orthodox Church to study Koine Greek. During that time, our priest resigned his position at Saint Seraphim, and a young priest came from Saint Vladimir's seminary, I learned later, to set everyone straight with support of his bishop. Within one month of his tenure, he excommunicated 12 communicants, including the entire Saint Seraphim choir. Soon the parish was again down to two or three families.

I spoke to one Antiochian priest about the matter who said the priest did it all wrong. What he should have done would have been to quietly ask each one separately to renounce their abomination and excommunicate them one at a time. That way he would not have to contend with the wrath of the congregation.

As it was in St. Seraphim, half the congregation supported the gays to no avail. One year later, the young priest was defrocked for some reason unknown to me. But what happened to the spiritual lives of all the members?

After this separation from my spiritual community, I personally fell into a deep, chronic, clinic depression that lasted years. I finally got sober though the spiritual exercises of Alcoholics Anonymous and through the loving, caring and sober friends I met there. I have a renewed faith now in the Orthodox Church and a trust in God that is unshakable.

I often, however, experience mainline Orthodox Churches as "cold" and unloving to me, even though the Orthodox Church is the Historic Church that I had been searching for so many years. My formation at Saint Seraphim Orthodox Church in a truly loving, caring and honest Orthodox community was too deep to find a substitute home or to simply hide myself, as others somehow have been able to do. I deeply miss my Orthodox friends.

THE FOUNDING OF AXIOS IN LOS ANGELES

Axios was founded in 1980 in Los Angeles, California. We met once a month with forty members for Vespers followed by a potluck dinner and meeting to discuss our situation. We regularly participated in the West Hollywood Pride festival, distributed information through the, then, "Religious Gay Coalition," and even had our own red tee shirts. But after three years of Axios solidarity, one of two members, entrusted with the Axios mailing list and publication of the Axios newsletter, started insisting that we expulse the two or three Eastern-rite Roman Catholic members that we had. This person had, in the past, been asked to leave by the Melkites, so he, seemingly, had some grudge with the Roman Catholics. Axios, as a group, does not celebrate Divine Liturgy. So the membership unanimously, except for the two, voted to reaffirm full membership of Eastern-rite Roman Catholics. The two newsletter editors were furious and sent our entire confidential mailing list to the bishop in San Francisco. The bishop in San Francisco sent down letters to all the clergy advising them to not serve Holy Communion to Axios members and also to discontinue the practice of "general confession" which was allowing gays to avoid being "confronted" in Confession.

Now it should not be assumed that most Orthodox clergy actively seek out gays and refuse to serve them. In fact, the real attitudes of priests towards homosexuality have ranged all over the place as I have spoken to them. In confession, some say, "Do not confess anything you do not believe is a sin." Others say that it is a sin but no worse than gluttony as they point to their own stomach. Still others call it an abomination and condemn devout gay lovers who have been loyal together much longer than straights often do in our society. This last kind of priest presumably thinks that having a devoted lover leads to committing an abomination more often and expects the non-straight Orthodox Christian to throw away their lover. How many gays and others have given up on the Orthodox Church because of this false orthopraxis as well as lack of transparency and consistency?

My repeated attempts to restart Axios meetings in Los Angeles have been met with fear from the former members who have said, "Remember what happened the last time." That seemed to work for those who are comfortable hiding themselves from everyone. Some of us eventually come to see honesty, integrity and dignity as essential attributes of the word "Orthodoxy". Can "right worship" be possible where truth is hidden? The "clobber passage" most often used by many priests to justify throwing away one's lover is the story of Sodom and Gomorrah, which actually describes intended violence not love. Since the story is actually about rape instead of love, it seems obvious that these were heterosexuals trying to humiliate the strangers. If this fallacious argument actually worked then it would condemn all straights and not non-straights. It is a silly pretense of an argument but still prominent on many Orthodox websites.

AXIOS CARRIES THE BATON UNDERGROUND

Around 1990, I realized that our situation had become steadily worse. With help from New York, but no help from any former members of Axios in Los Angeles who were in hiding, I decided to do what I could to be helpful to non-straight Orthodox Christians who wanted to find safe and Orthodox places to worship God "in sincerity and truth." I could never get a quorum together to start meetings again because those who practice "don't ask, don't tell" in the Orthodox parishes told me, "It is no one's business what I do in bed." I had hoped, instead, that they would find solidarity with gays who have a real need to be honest, at least with everyone with whom they share the Holy Kiss in Church. Here the reader might think I am dismissing all those gays who actually believe what is taught by the mainline churches in their official websites that gays must "bear their lifelong crosses" and never have a lover no matter how loving. Gays must immediately go to confession when they fall in love. Well I have spoken with and written to hundreds of Orthodox straights, Orthodox lesbians, Orthodox gay men as well as many clerics in these 20 years of underground activity. I try to send those who ask to Orthodox Churches who will serve them. Out of all these people who just want to worship God in peace, I only remember 2 or possibly 3 who believed this guidance was actually Orthodox and must be followed. I never attempted to interfere with their understanding in the matter. All the rest I know follow the "it is no one's business what I do in bed" approach or have left the Church.

FINAL THOUGHTS

It is, in fact, not spiritually safe to hide yourself from those to whom you give a Holy Kiss. Being honest and transparent has always been at the root meaning of the word Orthodox and also of the coming out process itself. Gays who are out hold the greatest paraenetic truth that can be given back to the Church. In the process, the Orthodox Church can recover its love for honesty and transparency which mark the Truth. However no one should be pushed to come out before they are ready. The history of Axios demonstrates that only in solidarity can we help each other find the Holy Orthodox communities that practice hospitality to all. Let us all pray and work for the day when we will be safely able to worship and be served in all Orthodox Churches with honesty, transparency and the non-judgmental love of God that is truly Orthodox.

FATHER GEORGE BATTELLE has been the representative of Axios in California for over twenty years. He served for five years as parish editor and choir member at Saint Seraphim of Sarov Orthodox Church in Long Beach, California. Now he serves as pastor of Saint Seraphim of Sarov Russian Orthodox Mission (saint-seraphim.org) in Hayward, California, a Russian Orthodox Mission under the omophorion of Bishop Symeon Ioannovskij, metropolitan of the Russian Orthodox Church in America (russianorthodox.org). He can be reached at fathergeorge@axios.org.

STUDY OF HOLY SCRIPTURE
BY JUSTIN R. CANNON, M.DIV.

REPRINT FROM "THE BIBLE, CHRISTIANITY, & HOMOSEXUALITY"

INTRODUCTION

This study is the product of years of research, dialogue, and prayerful reflection. It began when I decided that I needed to know once and for all what the Bible says about homosexuality. There are so many opinions floating around these days about what the Bible does and does not say about homosexuality. Some say, "The Bible clearly condemns homosexuality." Others assert, "Jesus abolished the law and said nothing about homosexuality– if it was so bad wouldn't he have said something?"

There are many fine books on the subject, but not everyone has the time or motivation to read a one hundred plus page book on this topic. Further, there are many cursory pamphlets on this topic, which really do not do the scriptures justice. My hope in writing this was to be comprehensive, yet also concise. Through this study, I offer you a close analysis of the Bible verses that have often been cited in contemporary times with reference to homosexuality. I will also explore homosexuality within the context of Christian tradition.

TERMINOLOGY

HOMOSEXUAL

The English word *homosexual* is a compound word made from the Greek word *homo*, meaning "the same," and the Latin term *sexualis*, meaning "sex." The term *homosexual* is of modern origin, and it was not until about a hundred and fifty years ago that it was first used. There is no word in biblical Greek or Hebrew that is equivalent to the English word homosexual. The 1946 Revised Standard Version (RSV) New Testament was the first translation to use the word homosexual.

SODOMITE

There is no word in biblical Greek or Hebrew for "sodomy" or "sodomite" as these terms have been used in contemporary times. A Sodomite would have been simply an inhabitant of Sodom, just as a Moabite would have been an inhabitant of Moab. Any translation of New Testament passages that make use of the words *sodomy* or *sodomites*, other than to simply refer to inhabitants of the town, are clear interpretations and not faithful translations.

LOOKING AT THE BIBLE

There are six Biblical accounts that have been used by some in recent times in reference to homosexuality. These include:

Genesis 1-2	*(Creation Account)*
Genesis 19:1-9	*(Sodom Account)*
Leviticus 18:22, 20:13	*(Holiness Code)*
Romans 1:24-27	*(Letter of Paul)*
1 Corinthians 6:9	*(Letter of Paul)*
1 Timothy 1:10	*(Letter of Paul)*

PASSAGE I: GENESIS 19:1-9
THE SODOM ACCOUNT

The story of Sodom is an appropriate text to begin with, as it has taken a central role in the study of homosexuality. We must first understand the context of this account. God, according to this account, sent two angels to warn Abraham's nephew, Lot, about the approaching destruction of Sodom. If we stop here for a moment we will see that even before sending the angels, God had intended to destroy Sodom. Whatever the reason was for the city's destruction, it had to do with the sin of Sodom before this event.

The angels came to the city of Sodom and Lot welcomed them to his home and prepared a meal for them. Then a grouping townsfolk, including the men, surrounded the house and asked where the angels who had come to the house were. They basically shouted, "Where are those men who came to your house? We want to have sex with them!" Lot refused, but offered his daughters instead, giving the reason: "Look, I have two daughters who have never slept with a man. Let me bring them out to you, and you can do what you like with them. Don't do anything to these men, for they have come under the protection of my roof" (19:8). The crowd insisted on what they wanted and tried to break through the door. The angels ended up pulling Lot into the house and blinding the crowd.

First of all, in interpreting this event we must take into account the entire situation. Whatever is happening here it is a form of rape. The crowd wished to sexually assault or "gangbang" the angels. The situation is, above all, sewn through with appalling violence. Many assert that Lot's offer of his daughters instead of the male angels implies that homosexual sex would have been worse than heterosexual sex, but Lot himself gives his reason for his action: "Don't do anything to these men, *for they have come under the protection of my roof.*" In our time, this does not make sense at all, but in Lot's day, hospitality was a nearly sacred contract, and it is that distinction that Lot expresses: *the visitors are his guests.*

In addition to the plain context of this story, namely that of rape, there are a few additional elements that shed some light on the fact that this story has nothing whatsoever to do with homosexuality.

For one, it is often asserted, that Genesis 19:4 depicts solely the men of the town sexually pursuing the angels. An example of this would be the New International Version (NIV) of the Bible that reads, "Before they had gone to bed, all the men from every part of the city of Sodom—both young and old—surrounded the house." If you look at the original Hebrew text, and even early Greek translations, the word translated into English as "men" can be inclusive of the women as well, much like the historical, antiquated use of the term "man" or "mankind," or the Spanish third person plural *ellos* and French *ils*. This is somewhat rendered in the King James Version (KJV), which translates this verse, "But before they lay down, *the men of the city, even the men of Sodom*, compassed the house round, both old and young, all the people from every quarter" (italics mine). In other words, it wasn't just the men of the city, but all the inhabitants, men and women, young and old alike.

Even in light of this, even if somewhere were to still claim that the distinction is gender-based, he or she could only assert that homosexual rape of angels is worse than heterosexual rape. To use this story to condemn loving, committed, monogamous homosexual relationships is unfounded and truly stretching this story outside of its historical framework, but that is exactly what has happened. As Jeffrey S. Silker, in reference to such distortion of this text, wrote in his article in *Theology Today*, "As for the Sodom and Gomorrah story, one can certainly conclude that homosexual rape (just like heterosexual rape)…is an abomination before God, but it does not follow from this that all expressions of homosexuality are prohibited (David's sin of adultery with Bathsheba does not make all heterosexual expressions sinful!)."[1]

If we are left wondering, then, what the sin of Sodom really was— so horrendous that God had decided to destroy the town— we only need to look to Ezekiel 16:49-50. The NIV Bible, one of the more evangelical translations of the Bible, renders these verses: "Now this was the *sin of your sister Sodom*: She and her daughters were arrogant, overfed and unconcerned; they did not help the poor and needy. They were haughty and did detestable things before me. Therefore I did away with them as you have seen." Other translations are equally revealing, and just as explicitly lay out the *sin of Sodom* as inhospitality, greed, and arrogance. These are the sins of Sodom.

If that is not convincing enough, let us look to the words of none other than Jesus himself in the Gospel of Luke. When he sent out his disciples, he compared the fate of the *inhospitable* towns that would not receive them to the fate Sodom, saying that it will be worse off for these towns that do not welcome the disciples. He explains, "Whenever you enter a town and its people welcome you, eat what is set before you; cure the sick who are there, and say to them, 'The kingdom of God has come near to you.' But whenever you enter a town and they do not welcome you, go out into its streets and say, 'Even the dust of your town that clings to our feet, we wipe off in protest against you. Yet know this: the kingdom of God has come near.' I tell you, on that day it will be more tolerable for Sodom than for that town" (Luke 10:8-12, RSV).

The sin of Sodom was that of greed, inhospitality, rape, and arrogance. In no way can this account be read with reference to homosexuality, much less loving, committed, homosexual relationships.

AN INTERESTING FACT

In the 1508 Wycliffe translation of the Bible into Middle English, the Greek word *arsenokoites* (ἀρσενοκοίτης) in 1 Corinthians 6:9 was translated "synn of Sodom." Wycliffe's own interpretation was that *arsenokoites* had something to do with the Sodom story, though nothing is implied as such in the New Testament text. The author could very well have written "sin of Sodom" if he had wanted to.

If your Bible translation has the translation "sodomites," it is an interpretation and not a faithful translation. We will look more closely at the word *arsenokoites* below in our study of the 1 Corinthians and 1 Timothy texts; however, it is remarkable to see how the story of Sodom, filled with rape and violence, has taken such a central role surrounding the topic of homosexuality and more precisely in the development of the word "sodomite" to what it means today.

IMPORTANT TERM : ARSENOKOITES (ἀρσενοκοίτης)

This Greek noun is formed from the joining together of the Greek adjectival prefix for male (*arseno-*) and the Greek word for beds (*koites*). Literally then it would mean, "male beds." It is found in 1 Timothy 1:10 and 1 Corinthians 6:9. This is the first appearance of the word in preserved Greek literature, and outside of these two verses this word does not appear at all in the Bible.

The meaning of the word *arsenokoites* in both *1 Corinthians 6:9 and 1 Timothy 1:10* is debated. Because of the obscurity of this word and the lack of outside sources to shed light on its meaning, we must derive its meaning from the text.

PASSAGE II: 1 TIMOTHY 1:8-10

> "*Now we know that the law is good, if any one uses it lawfully, understanding this, that the law is not laid down for the just but for the lawless and disobedient, for the ungodly and sinners, for the unholy and profane, for murderers of fathers and murderers of mothers, for manslayers, immoral persons, sodomites, kidnappers, liars, perjurers, and whatever else is contrary to sound doctrine…*" (RSV)

The word translated as *sodomites* in the list above is none other than the Greek word *arsenokoites*. Right now we should ask, "What exactly does this word mean?" Just as you or I might do when going shopping, it is not uncommon when writing lists to group common things together. If you look closely at 1 Timothy 1:9-10, you can see that there are structural pairs that are reflected below in the English as well as in the Greek– the original language of the New Testament:

1 TIMOTHY 1:9-10 (RSV) – ENGLISH

Row A:	lawless	and	disobedient
Row B:	ungodly	and	sinners
Row C:	unholy	and	profane
Row D:	murderers of fathers	…of mothers	manslayers
Row E:	immoral persons	sodomites	kidnappers
Row F:	liars	perjurers…	

1 TIMOTHY 1:9-10 (RSV) – GREEK
The Greek is provided for reference purposes only.

Row A:	ἀνόμοις	καὶ	ἀνυποτάκτοις
Row B:	ἀσεβέσι	καὶ	ἁμαρτωλοῖς
Row C:	ἀνοσίοις	καὶ	βεβήλοις
Row D:	πατρολῴαις	μητρολῴαις	ἀνδροφόνοις
Row E:	πόρνος	ἀρσενοκοίτης	ἀνδραποδιστής
Row F:	ψεύστης	ἐπίορκος…	

As you will notice in either chart, there is an obvious relationship between the words in each row. The chart below illustrates how the words in each row are either synonyms or closely related in some manner:

Row A:	*lawless* & *disobedient*	= two synonyms
Row B:	*ungodly* & *sinners*	= two synonyms
Row C:	*unholy* & *profane*	= two synonyms
Row D:	*murderers of fathers, murderers of mothers, manslayers*	= three types of murderers
Row E:	*Immoral persons, sodomites, kidnappers*	= ? (see next page)
Row F:	*liars & perjurers*	= two synonyms

93

The relationship between the words in rows A–D and row F are evident, but what about Row E? What do "immoral persons, sodomites, and kidnappers" have in common? To answer this question beyond a shadow of a doubt, we will need to explore the Greek. The three Greek words present in line E are: *pornos* (πόρνος), *arsenokoites* (ἀρσενοκοίτης), and *andrapodistes* (ἀνδραποδιστής).

Some commonly read Bible translations include the King James Version (KJV), New International Version (NIV), New King James Version (NKJV), Revised Standard Version (RSV), and New English Bible (NEB). These words were, respectively, translated in the following manner:

	pornos	*arsenokoites*	*andrapodistes*
KJV:	whoremonger	"them that defile themselves with mankind"	men-stealers
NIV:	adulterers	perverts	slave traders
NKJV:	fornicators	sodomites	kidnappers
RSV:	immoral persons	sodomites	kidnappers
NEB:	fornicators	perverts	kidnappers

As we see there is no clear-cut agreement as to what these words mean, though the above translations agree on the general sense of such words. To determine the precise meanings of these words, we will use a lexicon. A lexicon is a scholarly dictionary used to determine the general meaning of biblical words. A search through the a Greek lexicon gives the following information on the Greek term *pornos*, the first of the three words:

Pornos derives from the verb *pernemi* meaning "to sell" and the following three definitions are given:
　　1.　a male who prostitutes his body to another's lust for hire
　　2.　a male prostitute

3. a male who indulges in unlawful sexual intercourse, a fornicator

Andrapodistes, the third word, returns the following definitions:
1. slave-dealer, kidnapper, man-stealer
   a. of one who unjustly reduces free males to slavery
   b. of one who steals the slaves of others and sells them.[2]

Arsenokoites, as previously indicated, is made up of the Greek words for male (*arseno-*) and beds (*koites*). In Greek, the word *koitai*, literally meaning beds, is commonly used as a euphemism for one who has sex. *Arseno-* is an adjectival prefix, thus literally we could translate this as "a man who has sex" or "male bedder."

We have, first of all, a male prostitute, the "male-bedder" (*arsenokoitai*), and the slave dealer. The New American Bible offers a footnote that might shed some light on the historical context of the time:

"The Greek word translated as boy prostitutes designated catamites, i.e. boys or young men who were kept for purposes of prostitution, a practice not uncommon in the Greco-Roman world. In Greek mythology this was the function of Ganymede, the "cupbearer of the gods," whose Latin name was Catamus. The term translated practicing homosexuals refers to males who indulged in homosexual practices with such boys…" (New American Bible, footnote for 1 Corinthians 6:9 where *arsenokoites* is also used).[3]

It was a common practice for men of Paul's time to have slave "pet boys" whom they sexually exploited. Dr. Ralph Blair explains, "The desired boys were prepubescent or at least without beards so that they seemed like females."[4] Today, this practice is referred to as pedophilia. Regardless, we know that the *pornos* is a prostitute, and most probably a young boy prostitute.

Keeping this in mind, let's look back at what we have so far: the young male prostitute, the "male-bedder" (*arsenokoites*), and the slave dealer. This contextual dynamic leads one to understand *arsenokoites* as being the one who sleeps with the prostitute—the man who literally lies on the *bed* with him. It is as if Paul were saying, "male prostitutes, males who lie [with them], and slave dealers [who procure them]."[5] Not only does the syntactical and historical context point to this understanding, but also the very literal sense of the word *arsenokoites* itself.

If this translation of *arsenokoites* is correct, it should also make logical sense where it is also used in 1 Corinthians 6:9, either confirming or refuting this understanding of *arsenokoites*.

PASSASE III: 1 CORINTHIANS 6:9-10

> *"Do you not know that the unrighteous will not inherit the kingdom of God? Do not be deceived; neither the immoral, nor idolaters, nor adulterers, nor sexual perverts, nor thieves, nor the greedy, nor drunkards, nor revilers, nor robbers will inherit the kingdom of God." (RSV)*

The term translated "sexual perverts" above is actually two different words. The first word is *malakoi* and the second term is that mysterious word *arsenokoitai* (Gr. ἀρσενοκοῖται). Some commonly read translations are as follow:

	malakoi	*arsenokoitai*
KJV:	effeminate	abusers of themselves with mankind
NIV:	male prostitutes	homosexual offenders
NKJ:	homosexuals	sodomites
RSV[1977]:	sexual perverts	
RSV[1989]:	male prostitutes	
Jerusalem:	catamites	sodomites

The term *malakoi*, as an adjective, literally means "soft." In Matthew 11:8 it has been used as an adjective in reference to John the Baptist's clothing. In this text, however, it is used as a noun and its meaning is debated. Does our understanding of *arsenokoitai* as revealed in 1 Timothy 1:10 as "men who sleep with boy prostitutes" make sense next to this word *malakos* which is translated by both NIV and RSV as *male prostitutes*? The Jerusalem Bible even translates the term *malakos* as catamites, those young *soft* prepubescent "pet boys" mentioned earlier.

The syntactical and historical context of 1 Timothy 1:10 reveals the meaning of the word *arsenokoitai* as men who sleep with boy prostitutes, and the fact this also fits the context of 1 Corinthians 6:9 seems to confirm that we have found the meaning of these obscure words. It makes perfect sense that Paul would rebuke not only the prostitute, but also the "male-bedder" or the man who sleeps with that prostitute.

As we see, these two verses are about this practice of prostitution and possibly pedophilia, but what about Romans 1:27? It clearly says, "...and the men likewise gave up natural relations with women and were consumed with passion for one another, men committing shameless acts with men and receiving in their own persons the due penalty for their error." Is this not clear enough? How are we to understand this?

PASSAGE IV: ROMANS 1:24-27

24	*Therefore God gave them up in the lusts of their hearts to impurity, to the dishonoring of their bodies among themselves,*
25	*because they exchanged the truth about God for a lie and worshiped and served the creature rather than the Creator, who is blessed for ever! Amen.*
26	*For this reason God gave them up to dishonorable passions. Their women exchanged natural relations for unnatural,*
27	*and the men likewise gave up natural relations with women and were consumed with passion for one another, men committing shameless acts with men and receiving in their own persons the due penalty for their error.* (RSV)

To understand what exactly Paul is writing about, we must look at the event as a whole and not isolate a mere portion of it. Each verse in this story gives us a glimpse into the situation.

Verse 24: "Therefore, God gave them up in the *lusts of their hearts* to impurity." If we are painting a picture of this account, it begins with the image of LUST.

Verse 25: "…they exchanged the truth about God for a *lie* and *worshiped and served the creature* rather than the Creator." Now there is a LIE as well as IDOLATRY involved (i.e. worshipping something other than God).

Verse 26: "God gave them up to *dishonorable passions*…" Now DISHONORABLE PASSIONS are presented. Looking back at this now we see this as a situation of lust, lies, idolatry, and dishonorable passions.

Verse 26 and 27 continue: "Their women exchanged natural relations for unnatural, and the men likewise gave up natural relations with women and were consumed with passion for one another…"

Looking at the men first will help to clarify the passage: "The men likewise gave up natural relations with women…" It is easy to overlook what this is saying because of the interpretation that has been ingrained into our minds through poor teaching, but read that carefully. They *gave up* natural relations with women, and then had sexual relations with on another. There is a movement from A) having natural relations with women to B) giving up those relations and having sexual relations with men. The word translated as "gave up" is the Greek word *aphentes* (ἀφέντες) meaning: *to give up, leave behind, forsake, or divorce*. The question must be asked: How can you give up something you do not have? How can you divorce yourself something you are not bound to?

The men Paul was writing about, he explains had what was regarded for them as natural relationships with women. Basically, today we would say these were heterosexual men— men who are naturally sexually attracted to women. These men, we see, turned their backs on their wives and were consumed with passion for one another. The women in the account did likewise.

Why would these men do that? As any biblical scholar will tell you: "Context is everything." This is a situation of lust, falsehood, idolatry, and dishonorable passions. In this account there are a number of men and a number of women. Both an accurate reading of this text, and a little historical knowledge would identify this situation as an orgy, not uncommon in the Greco-Roman world. Just look at the language: everyone is filled with lust and "dishonorable passions" having sex with whomever, however.

But why would Paul be talking about orgies? A little research into pagan religious practices contemporary to Paul uncovers the pagan practice of "sacred sexual orgies." Baal was the Canaanite deity that was worshipped with sexual orgies on Mount Peor in Moab, a pagan practice with which Paul would have been familiar. Apparently, during these "sacred" orgies entire families would have sex with no regard for familial bonds, gender, or age. It makes complete sense for Paul to condemn such practices. With this contextual understanding let us read this story again:

> *"Therefore God gave them up in the lusts of their hearts to impurity, to the dishonoring of their bodies among themselves, because they exchanged the truth about God for a lie and worshiped and served the creature rather than the Creator, who is blessed for ever! Amen. For this reason God gave them up to dishonorable passions. Their women exchanged natural relations for unnatural, and the men likewise gave up natural relations with women and were consumed with passion for one another, men committing shameless acts with men and receiving in their own persons the due penalty for their error."*

Anyone who isolates verses 26 and 27 to condemn homosexual relations as unnatural is projecting their own prejudice into these verses and reading this letter entirely outside of context. Even if we were to isolate those verses, they could only be used to condemn heterosexuals who go against their own nature and engage in homosexual activity. As Peter J. Gomes, preacher to Harvard University, further clarifies in his book *The Good Book*, "It is not clear that Saint Paul distinguished, as we must, between homosexual persons and heterosexual persons who behave like homosexuals, *but what is clear is that what is 'unnatural' is the one behaving after the manner of the other*"[6] (italics mine). Interestingly enough, one could argue, in light of this understanding that it would be a sin for a homosexual to engage in heterosexual sex.

So far we have looked at all three of the New Testament scriptures that are often used in reference to homosexuality as well as the Genesis narrative about the destruction of the city of Sodom. That leaves us with two other scriptures that are mentioned when this topic is brought up: The Leviticus laws and the Creation Narrative.

PASSAGE V: GENESIS 1-2 (CREATION NARRATIVE)

"God created Adam and Eve, not Adam and Steve!" In so many places I have either read or heard the above refrain used by Christians trying to "prove" that homosexuality is wrong. You cannot really argue with them about God creating Adam and Eve in the Biblical creation account. In *that* sense, then, they are right. But, one must ask what exactly is revealed by this Creation account. In *The Good Book*, The Rev. Peter Gomes writes the following concerning the creation narrative:

> "...*the authors of Genesis were intent upon answering the question 'Where do we come from?' Then, as now, the only plausible answer is from the union of a man and a woman... The creation story in Genesis does not pretend to be a history of anthropology or of every social relationship. It does not mention friendship, for example, and yet we do not assume that friendship is condemned or abnormal. It does not mention the single state, and yet we know that singleness is not condemned, and that in certain religious circumstances it is held in very high esteem.*"[7]

In other words, the relationship of Adam and Eve is the only relationship that would make sense for a account on creation. This is a story about where humanity came from, and only a procreative relationship (i.e. heterosexual) would be appropriate for this particular story. This does not mean a procreative relationship is for everyone, or that God intends such for every, just because that is the source of humanity. Keep in mind that many of the saints and even Jesus lived a solitary, celibate life that does not conform to the model of the creation account. As such, we must read this account for what it is and not as an anthropology of all human relationships. If someone, in spite of this, were to base his or her opinion of homosexuality on the Creation story alone, their stance would not only be out of context, but also based on a weak argument.

PASSAGE VI: LEVITICUS 18:22

Common translations of Leviticus 18:22 include:

> "Thou shalt not lie with a man as with a woman; it is an abomination." (KJV)

> "Do not lie with a man as one lies with a woman; that is detestable." (NIV)

> "Homosexuality is absolutely forbidden, for it is an enormous sin." (*Living Bible*)

First of all I must point out how the quote above from the *Living Bible* is obviously an interpretation and by no means could it be considered a translation. Beware of bibles that try to pass mere interpretation as supposed "translations" of the scriptures. In any serious study of Leviticus 18:22, one must look closely at the historical context of this law in order to understand what the original author was referencing. The book of Leviticus is a part of the Hebrew Law and contains everything from commandments for men not to shave the edges of their beards (Lev 19:27); orders not to have intercourse during menstruation (Lev 18:19); not to harvest different crops in the same field (Lev 19:19); as well as numerous dietary laws.

In order to understand this particular law we must look first at the Hebrew Law and how it relates to Christians, an issue the early church faced when Gentiles were being converted. Second, we will look at the eighteenth chapter of Leviticus as a whole, and particularly how this law is a part of the Levitical holiness code. Lastly, we will end this section with a careful examination of Leviticus 18:22.

LEVITICUS: THE LAW

The early church was faced with the question of whether or not the Levitical laws apply to Christians. Many Gentiles were being converted to Christianity, yet they were not circumcised, nor did they follow the Law that God had given to the Israelites. It was through the observation of the Law that the Israelites considered themselves justified before God. In reading Paul's letters to the Romans, the Galatians, the Corinthians, the Colossians, and the Hebrews we find a consistent claim that "no one is justified before God by the law" (Galatians 3:10). Paul writes the following in reference to the law:

> *"Likewise, my brethren, you have died to the law through the body of Christ, so that you may belong to another, to him who has been raised from the dead in order that we may bear fruit for God. While we were living in the flesh, our sinful passions, aroused by the law, were at work in our members to bear fruit for death. But now we are discharged from the law, dead to that which held us captive, so that we serve not under the old written code but in the new life of the Spirit"* (RSV Romans 7:4-6).

> *"Now before faith came, we were confined under the law, kept under restraint until faith should be revealed. So that the law was our custodian until Christ came, that we might be justified by faith. But now that faith has come, we are no longer under a custodian* [i.e. The Law]. *For in Christ Jesus you are all sons of God, through faith"* (RSV Galatians 3:23-26).

Other New Testament Scriptures on the Law include: 2 Corinthians 3:6; Colossians 2:13-15; Hebrews 8:8-13, Romans 10:1-4. In the second chapter of his letter to the Galatians he confronts Peter who has been forcing Gentiles to follow the Jewish law (Galatians 2:14), and he goes on to boldly assert:

> *"We ourselves, who are Jews by birth and not Gentile sinners, yet who know that a man is not justified by works of the law but through faith in Jesus Christ, even we have believed in Christ Jesus, in order to be justified by faith in Christ, and not by works of the law, because by works of the law shall no one be justified"* (RSV Galatians 2:15-16).

Paul was even persecuted for this deeply held conviction that as Christians, we are no longer held to the Levitical laws, but are justified through faith and sanctification in Jesus Christ.

If we are "not under the law" does that mean we can lie, cheat, steal, etc.? In Romans 6:15 Paul answers this question, "By no means!" Did not Christ himself in Matthew 5:17 say that he came not to abolish the law, but to fulfill it? So what is the fulfillment of the law? Jesus was once asked, "Rabbi, which is the greatest commandment in the law?" Jesus replied, "You shall love the Lord your God with all your heart, and with all your soul, and with all your mind. This is the great and first commandment. And a second is like it: You shall love your neighbor as yourself. On these two commandments depend all the law and the prophets" (Matthew 22:36-40). The fulfillment of all the law and prophets is the higher law of love, given to us by Christ. Paul would later echo this idea in Romans as he wrote:

"Owe no one anything, except to love one another; for he who loves his neighbor has fulfilled the law. The commandments, 'You shall not commit adultery, You shall not kill, You shall not steal, You shall not covet,' and any other commandment, are summed up in this sentence, 'You shall love your neighbor as yourself.' Love does no wrong to a neighbor; therefore love is the fulfilling of the law" (RSV Romans 13:8-10).

LEVITICUS: THE HOLINESS CODE

There are over 600 laws in the Old Testament and the book of Leviticus contains many of such laws (For a list of the 613 laws recognized by many contemporary Jews, visit jewfaq.org/613.htm). The book of Leviticus is a part of what is described as the "Holiness Code," which was given to protect the Israelites from idolatry and to distinguish them from pagan cultures.

Leviticus 18 begins, "And the Lord said to Moses, 'Say to the people of Israel, I am the Lord your God. You shall not do as they do in the land of Egypt, where you dwelt, and you shall not do as they do in the land of Canaan, to which I am bringing you. You shall not walk in their statutes. You shall do my ordinances and keep my statutes and walk in them. I am the Lord your God...'" (Leviticus 18:1-4). This introduction of Leviticus 18 clearly maintains that these laws were given to distinguish them from the ways of the people in Egypt and those in Canaan.

The Old Testament, as has been mentioned, was initially a part of the Hebrew Scriptures of the Jewish people. The *Septuagint* was an ancient translation of the Old Testament (circa 200 B.C.) from its original Hebrew into Greek. It was the "version" of the Old Testament that the New Testament writers often quoted when they cited Old Testament scriptures. The Hebrew word in Levticus 18:22 translated into English as "abomination" was translated in the *Septuagint* as the Greek word *bdelugma* (βδέλυγμα). A quick search through a lexicon for the word *bdelugma* brings up the following definition:

1. a foul thing, a detestable thing
    a. of idols and things pertaining to idolatry

This points to the understanding that this specific law has to do with a matter of ritual purity and with the Hebrews not being like the idolatrous Babylonians or Canaanites. It probably refers to either the sacred orgies involved in the worship of the god Baal, sacred temple prostitutes, or some other form of idolatry (see below).

LEVITICUS: ABUSIVE CULTIC PRACTICES

KJV: "Thou shalt not lie with a man *as with a women*; it is an abomination."

NIV: "Do not lie with a man *as one lies with a woman*; that is detestable."

Translated literally from Hebrew Leviticus 18:22 reads: *"And with a male you shall not lay lyings of a woman."* The only way of making sense of this is to insert something to produce a smoother, more coherent English translation. For example, one can insert "as the" or "in the" after the first *lay* as showed below:

> *"And with a male you shall not lay [as the] lyings of a woman."*
> *"And with a male you shall not lay [in the] lyings of a woman."*

Some affirm that this law is quite straightforward. Clearly from the previous sixteen verses, we know that these laws were written to men. Thus, some may say, this law forbids men to "lie with", or have sex with, other men. This interpretation is flawed as it entirely ignores the phrase "as with a woman." These four words cannot simply be understood to refer to lying sexually, since that is already indicated in the Hebrew word translated "to lie with." Since the verb translated "to lie with" already denotes sexual activity, if the above interpretation were what the author meant he could have just written, "Thou shalt not lie with a man; it is an abomination."

The phrase "as with a woman" must have been added for some reason, and we must understand the context of this law to understand it fully. The status of women in that time was much lower than that of men, and women were even considered property of their husbands.

Rabbi Arthur Waskow explains, "The whole structure of sexuality in the Torah assumes a dominant male and a subordinate female."[8] Further, in such patriarchal societies women were considered property of men, and were "obedient" to their husbands. In having sex, therefore, one should not be shocked that men would often have been dominating and controlling in sexual encounters.

For a man to be treated in that way (i.e. as a woman) within the Jewish culture of the time, the man would have be taking a lower status, as well as being sexually dominated and controlled. To do so would have been reducing him to property and in effect defiling the image of God, which man was considered in that culture. "Thou shalt not lie with a man *as with a woman*; it is an abomination" (KJV). Contextually understood, the meaning of this verse is clear. It is akin to saying: You shall not sexually use a man like property. You shall no sexually subjugate a man as one does with women.

This does not mean that the author is endorsing other forms of sex between men. We can tell from this study, though, that he is not writing about loving, committed, gay relationships. Rather, as would be expected, the author is writing about abusive sexual practices common in his day and age. Just as when you and I write critiques of our culture, we are writing about practices we see and familiar with. This Hebrew author would have been familiar with the male temple prostitutes, and the activity described is exactly how men would have treated the male temple prostitutes—in a controlling and abusive manner. That is also how individuals would have been treated in the sacred sexual orgies with which Baal was worshiped. They would have had sex with other men "as with a women"– using them in self-centered ways.

AN INTERESTING CONNECTION

Earlier, in this study, it was shown that Paul always uses the term *arsenokoites* following a word for a young boy prostitute (i.e. *pornos* in 1 Cor:6-9 and *malakoi* in 1 Tim 1:10). If we look closely at the Greek Septuagint translation of Leviticus 18:22 (circa 200BC), there is an interesting connection between this Levtical law and that unique term that Paul coined, *arsenokoites*.

The first phrase of Leviticus 18:22 reads as follows:

English	with	male	not	lay	bed	of woman
Greek	μετὰ	ἄρσενος	οὐ	κοιμηθήσῃ	κοίτην	γυναικός
	meta	arsenos	ou	koimethese	koiten	gynaikos

In the chart above, notice the close proximity of the words *arsenos* (Gr. ἄρσενος) and *koiten* (Gr. κοίτην). These two words, found merely two words apart from each other in this Levitical law, are the very words combined by Paul when he coined the term *arsenokoites* (Gr. ἀρσενοκοίτης). Our study of the term *arsenokoites* indicates that Paul used it to denote men who consorted with young boy prostitutes. I am convinced that Paul was looking at this law when he coined this term. His usage of the term indicates that he understood Leviticus 18:22 to be speaking of temple prostitution. This is consistent with our study of the cultural and social context of Leviticus 18:22, wherein men would have been using other men in a sexually exploitative manner, not unlike how the male temple prostitutes would have been "used" by the men who hired them. The compelling evidence is that an independent study of the context of Paul's letters and a study of the context of what it means to "lie with a man *as with a woman*" affirm the same understanding of what is being condemned by these passages—controlling sexual abuse or use of another man.

CONCLUSION ON LEVITICUS 18:22

As we see, this Levitical law is not as simple as it appears. First of all, we know from Paul's writing that we have "died to" and are "discharged from the law" (Romans 7:4-6). We also know that "love is the fulfilling of the law" (Romans 13:10). Second, we understand that Leviticus is a part of the Holiness code, which was written to distinguish the Israelites from the Canaanites and Moabites. Lastly, we see that Leviticus 18:22 has to do with abusive cultic practices, and says nothing pertaining the issue we are faced with today—that of loving and committed homosexual relationships.

SCRIPTURE STUDY CONCLUSION

As we see, the Bible really does not fully address the topic of homosexuality. In the city of Sodom, same-gender sexual behavior is mentioned within the context of rape (of angels), and in Romans 1:24-27 we find it mentioned within the context of idolatry (Baal worship) involving lust and dishonorable passions. Both 1 Corinthians 6:9 and 1 Timothy 1:10 talk about same-gender sexual behavior in the context of prostitution and possibly pedophilia, not uncommon in the Greco-Roman world.

Nowhere does the Bible come close to condemning a loving and committed homosexual relationship. To use the Bible to condemn such a relationship, as we see, involves a projection of ones own bias into the Biblical texts and a stretching of these texts beyond their original intent. Historically, though, the Bible has been taken out of context and twisted to oppress almost every minority one could imagine including women, those with mental disabilities, African Americans, children, slaves, Jews, and the list goes on. Do we truly understand the greatest commandments...

"You shall love the Lord your God with all your heart, and with all your soul, and with all your mind. This is the great and first commandment. And a

second is like it, You shall love your neighbor as yourself. On these two commandments depend all the law and the prophets." (RSV Mat. 22:36-40)

CHURCH TRADITION & MARRIAGE

Tradition, however, has held that marriage is a sacrament designed for a very specific purpose. The following is taken from the article *Homosexual Marriage* by Tex Sample and is reprinted with permission:

"To address Christian homosexual marriage, attention must be turned to the tradition of the church, and here I am indebted to the work of Daniel M. Bell Jr. St. Augustine is the major figure in the teaching of the church on marriage. For him marriage is an office, a duty in which one serves the church and the larger society. This office serves three ends. First is the procreative end, which is understood by Augustine as raising children for the Kingdom of God. It is not primarily having children of one's own in a biological sense. The second end is the unitive end in which couples learn faithfulness to each other and to God and become thereby witnesses to an 'order of charity.' The third is the sacramental end, which for Augustine relates more often to the indissolubility of marriage.

"These three ends are sustained in the later Middle Ages. While Augustine sees marriage as serving to restrain lust, in the later Middle Ages a more positive view develops in which marriage contributes to growth in holiness…

"The point is that marriage in the Christian tradition serves a number of ends: procreation, fidelity, sacramental, mutual support and companionship, mutual society, and loving companionship. What is striking is that all of these ends can be met by homosexual marriages, even the procreative end when the procreative end is understood as raising children for the Kingdom of God and not primarily as a function of nature [a biological function]. On these grounds, it is appropriate for gay and lesbian Christians to be married in the church, and it is not in violation of Scripture or tradition.

"The objection to this argument by some Christians is to raise up Mark 10:7-8 where Jesus states that 'For this reason a man shall leave his father and mother and be joined to his wife, and the two shall become one flesh.' The argument is then made that this is the only form scriptural marriage can take. The issue addressed in this passage, however, is divorce. Jesus is responding to a hard-hearted test of his authority. Extending his response to a blanket denial of homosexual marriage goes well beyond the text. Moreover, it is uttered by a single Christ who did indeed leave his mother and father to engage in his Incarnate mission. So long as we are dealing with a single Christ who left father and mother for a different reason, we must be open to other possible options, especially options that fulfill the ends of Christian marriage traditionally understood.

"In conclusion, biblical teaching does not address a host of same-sex practices, among them homosexual marriage. Moreover, the ends of marriage as understood in the tradition of the church are ends that homosexual marriage can fulfill. So the issue in the confirmation of a bishop in a homosexual relationship is not whether he or she is gay, not even whether he or she is a practicing homosexual. The question is: is he or she married to this partner, and if so, does this marriage meet these ends."[9]

THE "SACRAMENT" OF SEX

There are those who would say that the topic of homosexuality is really quite simple and just comes down to sex. They might ask, "Isn't the inherent function of sex procreation, an end which homosexual sex does not fulfill?" The 1958 resolution of the Ninth Lambeth Conference (the worldwide gathering of Anglican bishops), on the subject of intercourse affirmed:

> "*Sexual intercourse is not by any means the only language of earthly love, but it is, in its full and right use; the most intimate and the most revealing; it has the depth of communication signified by the Biblical word so often used for it, 'knowledge'; it is a giving and receiving in the unity of two free spirits which is in itself good (within the marriage bond) and mediates good to those who share it. Therefore it is utterly wrong to urge that, unless children are specifically desired, sexual intercourse is of the nature of sin. It is also wrong to say that such intercourse ought not to be engaged in except with the willing intention to procreate children.*"[10]

Sex within marriage can fulfill two divine functions: the procreative and the unitive. With regards to these two divine ends of sex (i.e. the procreative and the unitive), if you cannot fulfill one, does that mean you should not do the other? It is like asking, if you are sick and cannot go to church should you not pray? If homosexual sex can fulfill one of the two divine ends of sex, is that not reason enough to bless lifelong homosexual unions/marriages? Interestingly enough, many churches today permit the marriage of infertile couples, as well as the marriage of couples past childbearing age, both of which close the possibility of procreation. As Boston College Professor of Theology Charles C. Hefling, Jr. summarizes this beautifully: "Sex can be productive without being reproductive."[11]

CONCLUSION

As we have seen, Scripture does not really have much negative to say about the issue of faithful homosexual relationships, or homosexuality for that matter. Furthermore, we have come to see that homosexual sex within a marriage can fulfill one of the divine ends of sex (i.e. the unitive), and that such a marriage also fits within the traditional Christian understanding of the sacrament of marriage—an image of the fidelity and love between God and His Church. I would like to leave you with a short story adapted from an oral rendition by Natalie Graber:

Once there was an old man who had to carry water up the hill from the river to his house each day. One of his water jugs, however, had a crack in it, so that, by the time he arrived at the top of the path, most of the water was lost. His neighbors laughed at him: "Why don't you buy a new water jug?" Even his wife criticized him: "Why don't you buy a new water jug?" But the man said nothing.

One day, he said to them, "Come with me," and led them, skeptical but curious, down the path that ran from his back door to the river.

"Almost every day," said the man to his wide-eyed companions, "on my way to the river, I scatter seeds. On my way home, water leaks from my precious jug to nourish them."

To their amazement, the entire left side of path was in bloom. A riot of color—flowers of every hue and tone— made the path a paradise.

Could it be that homosexuality is similar to that second jug? It may appear broken from one individual's limited and restricted perspective, but truly what appears to be "brokenness" is indeed a hidden virtue. Could one even imagine that the jug is not necessarily "broken," but rather that God, out of abundance and creativity, created more than one type of jug for more than one purpose?

On another note, we accept that it is true that we are not only spiritual and mental beings, but also physical and sexual beings. Does it make sense then that a large percent of God's children should live in denial of a fundamental part of who they are? Should this group be forced to live without the affection and intimacy that comes with committed partnership? Nonetheless, that is precisely what is happening. Homosexuals in the Church are not only among the most marginalized groups, but are often victims of violence or driven to suicide because they cannot make sense of their sexual feelings in the light of what they believe or are told their Bible says. Or because of a lack of understanding of what the Bible truly says (or doesn't say) they are, more often than not, driven to leave the Church.

SOURCES CITED IN SCRIPTURE STUDY

[1] Siker, Jeffrey, "How to Decide? Homosexual Christians, the Bible and Gentile Inclusions." *Theology Today* 51 (1995), p.221.
[2] Thayer and Smith. "Greek Lexicon entry for Pornos". "The New Testament Greek Lexicon". Online at http://www.searchgodsword.org/lex/grk/view.cgi?number=4205.
[3] *The New American Bible* (World Bible Publishers, Inc., 1987), p.1236.
[4] Blair, Dr. Ralph. Available Online at http://www.ecinc.org/Scriptures/clbrpg.htm
[5] Scroggs, Robin. The New Testament and Homosexuality: Contextual Background for Contemporary Debate. (Augsburg Fortress Publishers, 1983), p.120.
[6] Gomes, Peter J. *The Good Book*. (William Morrow & Company, 1996), p.157.
[7] Ibid., p.49-50.
[8] Waskow, Arthur. *Homosexuality and Torah Thought*.
[9] Sample, Tex. *Homosexual Marriage*. Available Online at http://rmnetwork.org/marriage/resources/sample.pdf
[10] *The Family Today: The Report of Committee Five of the Lambeth Conference 1958 Together with the Text of Relevant Resolutions Passed by the Conference* (New York: National Council, Episcopal Church, 1958), p.13.
[11] Gomes, p171.

RESOURCES
FOR GAY ORTHODOX CHRISTIANS

Axios: Eastern & Orthodox Christians Gay Men & Women
http://www.eskimo.com/~nickz/axios.html
http://www.qrd.org/QRD/www/orgs/axios

Axios DC
http://axiosdconline.tripod.com
http://www.facebook.com/group.php?gid=17345109682
Axios DC: a fellowship of GLBT Eastern Christians in the national capital area for more than 15 years.

Axios Chicago
http://www.facebook.com/group.php?gid=105260255843
Private group for people interested in the Axios support group for GLBT Eastern Christians in Chicago.

California Gay Orthodox Christians
http://gayorthodoxchristian.multiply.com
Resource for GLBT Orthodox Christians with links, a blog, and other resources.

Ortodoksisen Sateenkaariseuran (Orthodox Rainbow Society)
http://sateenkaariseura.wordpress.com
Support group of gay, lesbian, and bisexual Orthodox Christian sponsored by the Finnish Orthodox Church.

Glory & Honor, Gay Orthodox Yahoo Group
http://groups.yahoo.com/group/gloryandhonour
Online "brotherhood" for gay and lesbian Orthodox Christians, though it does not seem very active.

The Gay Christian Network
http://www.gaychristian.net
This site has a message board with thousands of gay Christians from around the world. They also have an Eastern Orthodox Fellowship group on their message board.

Pro-Gay Orthodox Christians (and allies)
http://www.facebook.com/group.php?gid=20917659986
This group identifies as a fellowship for "Orthodox Christians who are disappointed by the church's view of gays and gay rights."

Inclusive Orthodoxy
http://www.inclusiveorthodoxy.org
My ministry to GLBT Christians, which highlights my bible study *The Bible, Christianity, & Homosexuality* in which I offer a close analysis of the seven scriptures often misused to condemn the GLBT community.

The Gay Map of the Orthodox World
OUT Traveler Magazine
http://gps.outtraveler.com/files/MapSummerHigh.pdf

Transsexualism and Eastern Christian Thought
http://sites.google.com/site/zoeshope
An informational website by a faithful male-to-female transsexual woman.

Being Gay and Coptic
http://gaycopt.blogspot.com
This is a blog by a gay, Coptic Orthodox Christian.

To purchase copies of this book, visit www.gayorthodox.com.